THE
AUDACITY
TO
WONDER

MARY ANN CLOYD

THE AUDACITY TO WONDER

A JOURNEY OF PERSISTENCE,
RESILIENCE, GRATITUDE, AND LOVE

Advantage | Books

Published by Advantage Books, Charleston, South Carolina.
An imprint of Advantage Media.

ADVANTAGE is a registered trademark, and the Advantage colophon is a trademark of Advantage Media Group, Inc.

Printed in the United States of America.

10 9 8 7 6 5 4 3 2 1

ISBN: 978-1-64225-604-8 (Paperback)
ISBN: 978-1-64225-603-1 (eBook)

Library of Congress Control Number: 2024918501

Cover & Layout design by David Taylor.

This publication is designed to provide accurate and authoritative information in regard to the subject matter covered. It is sold with the understanding that the publisher is not engaged in rendering legal, accounting, or other professional services. If legal advice or other expert assistance is required, the services of a competent professional person should be sought.

Advantage Books is an imprint of Advantage Media Group. Advantage Media helps busy entrepreneurs, CEOs, and leaders write and publish a book to grow their business and become the authority in their field. Advantage authors comprise an exclusive community of industry professionals, idea-makers, and thought leaders. For more information go to **advantagemedia.com**.

To my niece,

Dr. Trudi Cloyd.

Thank you for sharing your life and family with me.

*Never forget that you are amazing, and I love you
unconditionally—more than words can express.*

CONTENTS

A NOTE FROM THE AUTHOR XI

CHAPTER 1 1
WACO

CHAPTER 2 23
DALLAS

CHAPTER 3 41
LOS ANGELES

CHAPTER 4 51
JUST MARRIED

CHAPTER 5 59
BIG FISH, BIG POND

CHAPTER 6 75
DIVORCE COURT

CHAPTER 7 97
NEW YORK

CHAPTER 8 117
BETRAYAL

CHAPTER 9 129
HOME

ABOUT THE AUTHOR 141

ACKNOWLEDGMENTS 143

A NOTE FROM THE AUTHOR

This book recounts true events and stories as remembered by the author. To protect the privacy of individuals and entities involved, as well as the author, some names, characteristics, and identifying details have been changed, some events have been compressed, and some dialogue has been recreated. The essence of the stories remains authentic.

The author's intent in sharing these experiences is not to defame or disparage any individual or organization. Rather, this work aims to honestly portray the challenges faced by the author in her personal and professional life, highlighting many of the obstacles she encountered.

These accounts reflect the author's personal perspective and experiences. They are shared in the spirit of fostering understanding, promoting dialogue, and illuminating the complex realities faced by many in similar situations.

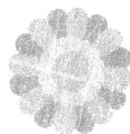

CHAPTER 1

WACO

I don't know how old I was when my mother left. No one told me. We didn't talk about it.

I never knew my mother. She left when I was an infant, and I have only vague memories of meeting her as a very young child. She and my dad divorced. I know that now, but that word was never used. I also knew that she had been pregnant once before me and that baby had died shortly after birth and is buried in a cemetery near where I grew up (the same cemetery where my grandparents, dad, and step-mother are buried today). That, people would talk about.

Everything else was a secret.

I remember a few years ago a then-friend telling me that she envied my life. I understood why she said this, and the comment was made in a kind way, noting all the incredibly interesting and fun aspects that make my life splendid and gratifying, perhaps enviable. But part of me wanted to say ...

"But you do not understand or appreciate all I have lived through to get here."

I am taking French lessons, and during one session my teacher was quizzing me about my family tree. It was striking to see on her whiteboard that I do not know almost half of me. On my mother's side, there was only *la mère*—no *la grand-mère* or *le grand-père*, no *la tante* or *l'oncle*. I do not know half my medical history. I know where I was born and where I grew up. But I don't really know where I come from.

I've come to accept the fact that I never will.

Today, as I write this from my Manhattan apartment, looking over the New York City skyline, I'm about a million miles (well, technically about 1,650 miles) from Mart, Texas—population just under two thousand. That's where I grew up and where most of the secrets were (and are) buried.

Mart is so quintessentially Texas that the first thing you see on the town website is that Mart is where "Champions are Made," likely referring to the local high school's multiple state football championships. However, as Texas as Mart was, I was not. I did not grow up wearing jeans or cowboy boots, I never have ridden or wanted to ride a horse, and to this day I have never held, much less shot, a gun. But those were just the superficial ways I was different. In fact, I was different all the way to the core of my being. And different is a really hard thing for any child to be.

I was different the minute my mother left me, as an infant, with my father. I was different because I lived with my grandparents instead of my parents. I was different because my father lived thirty minutes away, in Waco. I knew all this. I knew I was different. But because nobody talked about it, I didn't understand why or what it meant.

I was also different because I was Catholic in the middle of the Bible Belt, which was largely made up of Southern Baptists (who thought dancing was a sin) and the Church of Christ (which would not allow musical instruments in church). Mart also had a Methodist church and a Lutheran church, but you had to go to Elk or Waco to find a Catholic church.

My dad was so profoundly Catholic that, as a young man, he had studied to be a priest. Which was another thing nobody talked about. In retrospect, it may explain why, even though he and my mother divorced, and she remarried, moved to California, and had more children, he wore his wedding ring until the day she died.

While doing research for this book, I found my mother's death certificate. She died on December 26, 1961, at 10:06 a.m. in Oakland, California. She was thirty-five years old. Her birth date was November 11, 1926. I never knew her birth date before. I learned she was a legal secretary, the name of her second husband, and that he was an accountant. She was born in Minnesota (I always thought Wisconsin—maybe that is where she and my dad met or married). I also saw, for maybe the first time, the names of her parents.

I didn't know any of that when my dad came to tell me she had died. I remember him saying, "I will take you to the funeral if you want to go." I was a little girl, barely seven years old, and I did not want to go. I had never been anywhere in my life. I had never been on a plane.

I didn't even know her.

I lived with my grandparents instead of my dad, who had legal custody of me, which had to be virtually unheard of in Texas in the 1950s. There were not many other options for a single father who worked full time and had a baby to take care of. So his parents, my grandparents, stepped in and raised me. We lived in a small house in a not-great neighborhood with a washing machine on the back porch and peach, pecan, plum, and fig trees in the yard.

Just down the street, there was a woman who lived in what was essentially a shack, who made her living selling other people's old clothes. I would go to her house with some change to find clothes to play dress up, because my grandmother didn't really have anything that was suited to that activity. It pains me to say it, but unfortunately it is true—everyone called this woman N***** Annie. Yet somehow I was raised without prejudice in the South in the 1950s and 1960s. Once when I was a young girl, after hearing my grandmother use the N-word, my dad asked that she not use that word to refer to Black people. She responded by asking how he would feel if I married a Black man, except she again used that slur. My dad told her that he would much rather I marry a good Black man than a bad white man, noting that a man's race does not determine his character.

Today, I realize raising me had to be a labor of love for my grandparents—they were in their late fifties when they got me and were well into their sixties when I started school. But back then, they were just another thing that made me different. Even in my small-town school, my friends' parents were part of the PTA and got involved in different ways, especially the mothers. My grandparents did not.

Of course, I don't blame them. Raising a child at their age had to be exhausting. Which might explain why I also remember my grandmother sometimes saying, "Mary Ann, if you don't behave, we'll send you to an orphanage."

In my circumstances, this was an actual possibility. So I grew up feeling not only different but also profoundly, deeply afraid.

For the longest time, I was afraid to leave my grandparents. I remember being invited to slumber parties and literally crying and asking to go home before bedtime because I was so afraid. There was this part of me that always thought, *What if something happens to them while I am gone and I never see them again?*

They were not perfect, but they were the only security I had.

Growing up, I was quiet, shy, and very much an old soul. I remember being four or five years old and sitting around wondering, *What is a person, and why am I here?* Which I later learned from a therapist is not a normal thing for a child that age to think about. But I was always "that child." I remember when I was only twelve and at my cousin's home with a few other girls, and as everyone was talking about whatever twelve-year-old girls talk about, I was sitting alone, sobbing, because Virgil "Gus" Grissom, Edward H. White II, and Roger B. Chaffee died in a launchpad fire while preparing for the Apollo 1 launch. My friends did not understand. I do not know that they laughed at me, but I know they did not understand.

It's not that I was an outcast. I had friends. I was in the band. There was a lot of kindness around me; people cared and reached out and treated me well overall, but nothing could change the fact that I was just so different from everybody else. A lot of the time, I felt like I didn't belong to anybody or anything.

***

Once my mother died, my dad was free to remarry in the eyes of the Catholic Church, and he started dating. I remember him dating a widow who had children of her own, but when I was around eight and a half, he married Dorothy, who had never been married. When they told me, the first thing I asked was "Do I have to leave Grandpa and Grandma?" They assured me I did not. I was glad the choice was mine. My dad stayed in Waco with my stepmother, while I stayed in Mart with my grandparents.

Eventually, Daddy and Dorothy had a baby, Tommy, my half brother. My mother had children with her new husband—two girls that I was told about. One of these half sisters tracked me down more than once and tried to get me to participate in "family," but I would not. She would ask, "Aren't you curious?" I don't want to be mean or thoughtless, but honestly, I am not. It feels like another lifetime, and one that I don't look back on with great fondness.

Dorothy was not the evil stepmother of books and movies. She was a narcissist—not the malignant ones we read about today, but she had a way of making everything about her. I recall as an adult the two of us going to see either *Terms of Endearment* or *Steel Magnolias*, and as we were leaving and I made some comment about the daughter dying, her response was all about "that poor mother." I remember her commenting that my staying with my grandparents made it harder on Daddy (and her) because he felt like he still needed to come to Mart to see me. But that was as "difficult" as she got. She was very good to me and served as the mother figure in my life. She taught me to cook and sew and passed down her love of fashion.

Dorothy always had beautiful clothes. They were classic and elegant, and I believe they would be even today. She was a talented seamstress, although at the time I knew her, she bought most—if not all—of her clothes. I loved going to fabric stores with her and eventually became a very good seamstress as well. I was not the only girl in Mart who wore homemade clothes, but the clothes I made were probably more classic and high fashion. I would always pick the more complicated patterns—the *Vogue* patterns—and the more interesting fabrics.

While I tried to be stylish, I never thought of myself as attractive. I was overweight for a brief period before starting junior high, and I remember being teased about it, although it was just one more way I was different. However, when it was time to start junior high, which shared a building with the high school, I decided I needed to deal with it. I was so afraid of being teased by the older kids that I changed my eating habits and lost weight, which I never regained.

Still, I do not ever, ever, ever remember my father telling me I was attractive in any way, shape, fashion, or form. So I never felt attractive.

The one thing my father never failed to notice was my grades. I remember once saying, "Daddy, most parents would be thrilled to have a kid that got grades like I do."

He said, "Mary Ann, if all you were capable of was a C, I'd be very happy with that. I know what you're capable of."

I was always a top student, and to be honest, school came easily to me. I did my homework in front of the television all through school, even university. I was regarded as smart and promising, and everyone—my dad, my grandparents, my teachers, and my friends— expected that I would go to college. This was not necessarily the goal of most girls at Mart High School, but it was a given for me.

I was valedictorian of my class of forty-seven or so graduating seniors.

If you were a Texas girl in the 1970s, the main thing you expected and geared your life toward was getting married. I wasn't one of the popular girls, but I did have a boyfriend—he had once dated my cousin and was six years older than I. Back in those days, at least in my school, there were good girls and bad girls. And since he and I had had sex, I felt that I should marry him. What else was I going to do? I wasn't a bad girl.

Besides, if I had to get married, he seemed like not a bad option. He came from Mart—his father owned bulldozers and other heavy equipment and did excavation, land clearing, site preparation, and other similar work. But he was more sophisticated, at least to my eighteen-year-old mind. Not only was he older than I was; he had also graduated from college and was working for a very reputable accounting firm in Waco. And Waco had a country club and real restaurants and other things that Mart did not.

I don't remember the proposal or much about our dating life, but I vaguely remember shopping for the ring at the Zales jewelry store in the mall in Waco. We decided to get married immediately after I graduated high school, and when we sprung the news on Daddy and Dorothy, they tried to talk me out of it. My dad had saved money for me to go to college, even though he didn't come from much, and he told me, "Mary Ann, you could go anywhere."

That was nice in theory, but what did it mean? Baylor University was a good school, and it was right there in Waco, and I was getting married. So I graduated high school in May, started college and working part time in June, and got married in July.

My job was in Baylor's Department of Student Financial Aid and Placement, where the vice president of the department and all the full-time employees who worked for him loved having "local girls" because, unlike the students who came from out of town, we didn't go home to Dallas or Houston or out of state. We were available to work full time during the summer and holidays. Much of the work was administrative, often not challenging or interesting, and there are stories I still tell about the environment and comments that were made. But being on the inside of the department, I had a job and every grant and scholarship for which I was eligible. I don't think I ever paid tuition, and I never had a student loan. Plus, my ACT scores had placed me out of a whole semester at Baylor—all based only on what I learned in high school (Mart High School did not have Advanced Placement classes back in the 1970s, or test-prep training courses, or anything beyond sitting down and taking the test). With that free semester and going to summer school, all while working, I graduated in three years.

I had always been obsessed with the space program and had dreamed of working for NASA. There were no female astronauts back then, of course, but I had fantasized about becoming an engineer, or maybe going to medical school. However, when I got to college, I chose to study accounting—not because I had dreamed of being an accountant but because it was a pragmatic means to an end. I was a woman, it was the mid-1970s, I was in Texas, I was married, and I wanted to work. I asked myself, *What profession gives me a chance at a meaningful career?* Accounting seemed to be a good choice. My first husband, whom I will henceforth refer to as #1, and I got married on a Friday night in July and for our honeymoon took a weekend trip to the Dallas area and visited Six Flags Over Texas. Then I came back to work and school full time.

***

When #1 and I first got married, we lived in a small apartment near the Baylor campus. However, at some point during our engagement, he quit his accounting job and went into business with his dad. Eventually, he decided he needed to live closer to his job. So we moved into a very old duplex in Mart, and I commuted to Waco daily. I went to school and worked, and I also managed the cooking and the budget at home.

Baylor was quite an experience. It was and is a Southern Baptist university and therefore very conservative. My boss, Dr. H., the vice president of Student Financial Aid and Placement, was quite a character—and not just because he had to have his whole title included on any and every piece of correspondence. His wife, Mrs. H., also worked in the department. There was another full-time employee I'll call Mr. S., who was a go-to full-time employee of Dr. and Mrs. H., the one they included and trusted as much as they did anyone.

He was such a sycophant, always saying, "Oh yes, Dr. H. Yes, Mrs. H." Bless his heart …

I would sit in Dr. H.'s office, and he would talk and I would dutifully listen. He was lamenting one day about how others at Baylor, other vice presidents, had received more recognition than he did. Dr. So-and-so was being recognized for all he had done, and Dr. So-and-so was being recognized for whatever, and he looked at me and said, "But, Mary Ann, I don't worry about that. They may be getting their recognition now, but I know that I will get stars in my crown when I'm in heaven."

I just nodded and said, "Mm-hmm."

I had good grades and was a good student. One day during my senior year, Dr. H. called me into his office and said, "Mary Ann, I'm hoping that you will stay and work here." Even for the full-time people, in most cases it was a glorified clerical position, but he was serious. "Because, you know, Mary Ann," he continued, "while women have certain inherent talents like typing and filing, you're not really meant to be in the business world." One day recently, as I was putting away dishes, I thought back on this conversation. Can you imagine? Not only did this very senior and significant person at Baylor, the person who was in charge of the department that worked with companies to place students in the work world, not encourage or inspire me; he actually told me that I was limited by my gender!

I did take typing in high school, because I was advised that I might need it someday if I wanted a job. It has come in quite handy, actually. I drew the line at shorthand (although in retrospect, it might have been helpful in note-taking).

Still, Baylor was a school where more than 50 percent of the student body was female. I suspect many of those women were more interested in finding a husband than a meaningful career. I remember sitting in marketing class one day, and a girl across the aisle glanced over and saw the wedding ring on my hand. She looked at me and asked, "Are you married?"

I looked back at her. "Yes, I am."

"Why are you here?" she asked.

"To get a degree."

I found out I was Summa Cum Laude, among the top five in my class, when I walked into the graduation ceremony and looked at the program. Baylor might have had its idiosyncrasies, but I got a great education, and for that I will always be grateful.

All the "Big Eight" international accounting firms at the time came to campus to interview, and I interviewed with all of them. Had I been a man with my grades, I probably would have had every firm aggressively recruiting me. As it is, I only got one offer from a Big Eight firm, in Houston.

But #1 would not move to Houston, and I turned down the offer.

There was only one "second tier" national firm in Waco, and I interviewed there. Still, despite the fact that I had graduated Summa Cum Laude from a university in their very town, that firm did not make me an offer. When I interviewed with them, one of the partners, a gruff old guy, looked at me and said, "Mary Ann, you're married. If you have kids, who's going to take care of them?"

So I went to work for a local firm in Waco.

***

Soon after I graduated from Baylor, my grandmother got sick. She had started losing weight and went in for tests, and she had to have surgery. That was all we knew—obviously there was "something" they were operating on, but we did not know what that something was. We were all with her at Providence Hospital in Waco—Daddy and

Dorothy and Grandpa and me, and as I was holding her hand as they were wheeling her gurney away to take her to surgery, she looked at me and said, "Mary Ann, if this is cancer, I don't want to live."

The weekend before she went into the hospital, all of us and many of her friends were at her and my grandfather's house, no doubt for a meal. It was a happy visit.

The doctor came out after surgery and told us it was cancer. We must have looked surprised, because he looked at us and said, "You didn't know?" I do not know whether she had kept it a secret from us or if, when he told her, she did not process it as something that was really happening to her.

My dad asked, "Can we do chemo? Can we do anything?" And this wise, kind general surgeon said, "We could." But then he said, "If she did chemo, it might prolong her life by six months or so, and she would be miserable the entire time. She could not enjoy it." The doctor told us that the surgery should make her more comfortable and that her life expectancy was a few months.

She never made it out of intensive care.

They took her to the ICU after surgery, and she was there when my dad received a phone call in the middle of that night saying her kidneys had failed. We all rushed back to the hospital in the wee early hours of the morning. I was able to be with her all day, to hold her hand and talk to her and to tell this woman who'd raised me how much I loved her. She was not conscious, and I have no idea if she could hear me, but I talked with her as if she could, every word.

It was my first experience with intensive care, and I was not sure what would happen. We were there all day—we did not even leave to eat. The nurses were not only competent and professional; they were kind and compassionate. And finally, at some point that afternoon,

I looked at one of them and asked, "What should we do? How long is this going to last?"

"We don't know," she said. "This could go on for another two days or so."

We decided to take a break. Before we left, I told my grandmother one more time that I loved her, and since she was always worried that I was too skinny, I explained that we were all going to get something to eat and that we would be back in an hour or two.

We were walking through the door of my father's house, ten minutes away from the hospital, and the phone was ringing. She had literally died within minutes of our leaving her room.

It was the first time someone close to me had died. And she wasn't just close to me—she'd raised me. But somehow, seeing her in that state in the hospital and contrasting her with the woman I knew, who was vibrant and really enjoyed her later years, helped me separate the body from the soul of a person. I will always believe my grandmother did not want us there when she died. Recently, I was talking about this with an internist friend, and she told me this is not an uncommon story … although there are others, like my dear friend and onetime therapist, Lu, who told me I should write this book. Lu's fear was dying alone; she wanted to leave this earth surrounded by her loved ones, which she did. I like to feel that both these women, who were so important to me, got what they wanted.

While it was sad to lose my grandmother, I was completely at peace with it. That did not mean I didn't miss her—I can remember being back at their old house, the house where I grew up, and expecting her to walk in the door. But somehow I was granted the opportunity to go through losing someone who meant so much to me in a way that was a growth experience. After all, I was the little girl who was much, much older than she should have been before she was willing to spend a night away from her grandparents, the girl who used to obsess about them dying and wonder, *How am I going to deal with it? What am I going to do?*

I was able to say goodbye, just as I began my full-fledged adult life.

***

I worked for the local accounting and tax firm for a couple of years. I started out as a staff person, doing both tax and audit work, and I learned a lot and did well. I passed my exam and became a CPA, which was necessary if I wanted to be able to go far in my field. And then one day I looked around and realized, *I could be here in ten years doing almost the same thing I am doing right now.* I looked at the clients I was working with and the types of jobs I was working on, looked at the people above me … and I realized that even though I might get promotions and have people working under me, there was only so far I could go. And I wasn't even thirty.

The bigger firms, like the Big Eight firm that had offered me that job in Houston, had a lot more opportunities. There was the opportunity to progress, the opportunity for better training, the opportunity to see different types of clients, the opportunity to work on bigger projects, maybe even an opportunity to travel. Plus, the types of companies that were clients of those national and international firms were bigger and more interesting than the companies that worked with the local firm.

Somehow, I found out that Phil, the partner who had offered me the job in Houston, had moved to Waco and was teaching at Baylor. I called him and told him my name. I said, "I don't know if you'll remember me."

He said, "Mary Ann, of course I remember you," which was really nice to hear.

I explained my situation to Phil—that I had been working for a local firm, that it was a great firm and I had learned a lot, but that I felt I needed to move on and wanted more opportunity. I asked him if he could get me another interview at the Big Eight firm in Houston. He told me that not only could he do that; he was also consulting at the very same Waco-based national firm that had turned me down a few years before because they were worried about the possibility of my having a baby. Apparently they had gotten over that fear, because they let Phil let me know they were interested in interviewing me.

I went through the whole interview process again, this time with help from Phil and the benefit of a CPA designation and a few years of work experience. With Phil's help, I not only interviewed with that firm in Waco but was also flown to Dallas for an interview with another Big Eight firm. It was my first time on a plane, so it was unforgettable. It was on a commuter airline that flew between Dallas and Waco, a propeller plane, and the flight was not full—in fact, I may have been the only passenger. This was in the days before closed and locked cockpit doors. I told the flight crew, "Oh, wow, this is so exciting. I've never flown before," and the pilots invited me to the front of the plane to sit behind them to watch the landing into DFW. I probably did not even have a seat belt on! All I remember was thinking it was the coolest thing. And after all my travels, it still would be today. Imagine flying into DFW with a pilot's-eye view!

I received an offer from that firm in Dallas, but I also got an offer from the national firm in Waco that had turned me down. So once again, I made the decision not to put my marriage to that test and stayed in Waco. At least I was able to move from a local firm to a national firm, which nobody did in that day and age. I know it is common today, but back then it was virtually unheard of to go from one firm to another, of any size, for any reason. Once you had a job, you stayed there. I was ahead of my time.

My new employer was a national firm that worked with the premier companies in Waco. It was much bigger than the small, local firm where I'd started in terms of the number of partners and the number of people on staff, and because it was part of a large national firm, it offered much more sophisticated and in-depth training. I got to go to national training where I met people from other offices and was exposed to more sophisticated and complex challenges. I learned and I grew as a professional and as a person, rising to the level of manager.

***

The more time passed, the more I grew into my career and full-fledged adulthood, the more it became clear to me that I wasn't happy in my marriage. When I'd decided to marry #1, he was this older man who went to college and had a professional life. I was going to go to college and be a professional, and I had aspirations that we were going to move up and be in the upper echelons of Waco society. But #1 had backed away from all of that, going back to Mart and going into business with his father. We built a house on a golf course near Mart so he could be near work, but that business didn't always do well. In any given year, I was the one making more money—but I still had to do all the cooking and shopping too.

I was not sure what I wanted or expected, but I was sure it was not that.

From almost the very beginning of our marriage, when we were living in the apartment near Baylor, we fought, horribly and probably embarrassingly loudly—we were those neighbors that people hate to have living next door. It only got worse as the years passed. I started spending more and more time with my work colleagues. We would work a long, hard day, and after that we would leave work and go out for drinks in Waco, and I'd drive home. Yes, I'm embarrassed to say that now, but at least the roads weren't crowded. Besides, it was legal to drink and drive in Texas back then. The last drink you ordered at the bar was a "roadie" in a plastic cup.

I had affairs, including some with people I worked with. I was not trying to break up their marriages or my own; these were "safe affairs" with people who, like me, were unavailable. We were just looking for something to distract us from our respective situations.

***

Some of my colleagues and friends knew I was not happy in my marriage. Of course, when I looked around at the people I knew, I do not know that many—if any—of them were happily married. Maybe that is why I stayed with #1 for so long. But when I told a friend, who was the secretary one of my clients, that I couldn't stand for my husband to touch me, she recommended I make an appointment with a psychiatrist she was seeing, Bernie. Seeing a psychiatrist was not common back then, certainly not in Waco, Texas. But to this day, when a seemingly random opportunity presents itself, more often than not I will take it. So I made an appointment with Bernie.

And he probably saved my life.

Bernie was, like me, an outsider. He was from New York, Jewish, and living and working in Waco, Texas. I forget how he'd ended up there, but it had to be an interesting story. I told Bernie all about my marriage and my affairs and my life and my general unhappiness and dissatisfaction.

When we talked about my husband, I said, "I'm not sure if I love him."

Bernie said, "Mary Ann, you don't even *like* him!"

I must have looked shocked, so Bernie went on to say, "It's clear you can have sex with men you don't love, but you have to like them. Correct?"

I had to admit he was.

As I was walking out the door after our session, I asked him, "Does this marriage have any hope?"

I don't know exactly how he said it, but I distinctly remember what he said: "No." And I burst into tears. I think it was the first time my protective shield cracked.

Bernie, the Jewish psychiatrist from New York, was the first person I'd met that I felt understood me. Maybe because he was an outsider in Texas, it was easy for him to spot another one. He said to me, "Don't you see, you don't belong here? You don't fit in here. You never have fit in here. You never *will* fit in here." It was an epiphany for me. He opened my eyes to the point where, for the first time in my life, I felt proud of not fitting in. He helped me see that I had no choice but to move on.

It was, however, a very hard thing to do. You did not get divorced back then—at least, nobody in my circle did. Except, ironically, my very Catholic dad, who never talked about it or admitted it.

When I told my husband I wanted to leave, as miserable as we had been, he seemed genuinely surprised and devastated. He begged me to stay. He even called my best friend and begged her to beg me not to go. But I could not unsee what Bernie had shown me. I knew I had to leave not only my husband but Waco too. Not that I planned to start looking for a job out of town until after the divorce was final. I did not want anything to get in the way of my escape.

I remember absolutely dreading telling my dad and Dorothy. I do not remember if my husband was there with me, only that, after his initial resistance to the idea of divorce, he did nothing that was disruptive or mean or unkind. I do not remember telling his parents, so I assume he did that. My family was, of course, completely surprised, as I'd never given them any indication that anything was wrong. And then, at some point during the divorce process, my father wound up in a mental hospital.

I do not know what he did—I know now that my dad had suffered from severe depression for years, but that was another one of those things nobody ever talked about. I saw him almost every week. We would all go to church on Sunday and have lunch together afterward, and I remember that he would often, other than church and meals, spend all weekend in bed. From what I remember and know of him, I cannot imagine him ever doing anything violent. But Dorothy told me he'd started saying crazy things, or at least things that seemed crazy to her, so she called the sheriff's department and had my dad taken away to the psychiatric ward of the hospital.

Where he was given shock treatment.

When I told Bernie what had happened, his comment was "Maybe for the first time in his life, he's speaking up." But he did not get a chance to do that in any meaningful way. Instead of therapy, he got ECT (electroconvulsive therapy).

Dorothy blamed me for the whole thing. I do not remember her exact words, but how she viewed it was clear: *You getting divorced is what caused me to have to call the sheriff's department and have your dad taken off to have shock treatment.*

Family issues aside, I assumed the divorce itself would be simple, since luckily we'd never had children. I hired an attorney from one of the best firms in Waco, and since all I really knew about divorce was what I had seen in movies and on TV, being the woman in the situation, I expected to walk away with just about everything. But when I asked my lawyer, he looked at me and said, "Sorry, but I'm going to have a hard time playing you up as the helpless female." He told me I'd be lucky to get half.

In the end, #1 paid me around $15,000 to keep the house and his business, and I was free.

Around that time, a friend who was the wife of a client asked me to join her for a week in Hong Kong, where she was going on business. I had never been anywhere! My family had never traveled when I was growing up. A vacation would mean driving to Galveston or someplace else in Texas. So I said, "Sure, that'd be great."

I fell in love with Hong Kong. What a fabulous city. And I fell in love with travel—although I would not have time for much of that until later.

On the flight back, there was a man sitting across the aisle from me, and we must have talked almost the entire way back. He was the CEO of a public company in Houston. He was married. We ended up having an affair, but it was more of an intellectual attraction where there was just enough chemistry to take it further, but not too far. If I was in Houston, I would let him know, and if he was going to be in my area on business, he would call me. But everything stayed within boundaries.

***

I did not start interviewing until the divorce was final, but almost the day it was, I contacted Phil, who had gone through his own divorce and moved to Dallas. Phil was working for a one of the Big Eight firms and got me an interview there, and he also helped me line up interviews at most of the Big Eight firms in Dallas. This time around, I didn't even bother with any of the smaller national firms.

I told the partner I worked for at the firm in Waco that I planned to leave. He had trained and coached me, and I think perhaps he was even a little bit in love with me, and he tried to talk me out of it.

"Mary Ann," he said, "you can stay in Waco and have the chance to be a very big fish in a little pond. If you go to Dallas, all you're going to be is a little fish in a big pond."

I had offers almost everywhere I interviewed, including one from Phil's firm. Phil knew my boss very well—he was the person who'd introduced me to him and helped me get the job in the first place. I told Phil what my boss had said to me.

Phil said, "Mary Ann, who's to say you can't be a big fish in a big pond?"

And with that, I had the courage to accept the job at a Big Eight firm in Dallas.

A few weeks before I left, a high school friend of mine had a baby, and while visiting her in the hospital, I told her I was divorcing and moving to Dallas. She was surprised. She said, "But that's a big city!" I remember responding that I would love living in New York. I have no idea where that came from. I had never even been to New York.

My friend's response? "But, Mary Ann, there are Yankees there!"

If she only knew where I ended up.

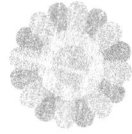

CHAPTER 2

DALLAS

I did not really know anyone in Dallas before I moved there. I did not have close friends from Baylor because I was married the entire time I attended. However, getting out of Waco was fantastic. I rented an apartment in a complex that was an easy drive to downtown. And I loved it. I loved having my own place. It was obviously smaller than the house I'd been in, but I did not care.

It was time for me to finally start living my own life.

I learned to scuba dive in Dallas, which is probably the last skill you would expect to pick up in a city located hundreds of miles from the nearest beach. The seed had been planted not long before I divorced #1, when we took a trip with friends to the Cayman Islands. We stayed on Seven-Mile Beach and went snorkeling. And there, I learned I do not like to hold my breath underwater. I could not figure out how to hold my breath and dive without the water coming down the snorkel. It was frustrating, because I loved what I saw and wanted to see more. So, sometime after I moved to Dallas, I took up scuba diving so I could breathe underwater.

I loved it. I loved it so much that I became certified through the rescue level. Not because I wanted to become a dive master but because I knew there was an element of diving that could be dangerous, especially when people panic. I wanted to be skilled enough to protect myself from stupid people.

I did my checkout dive in Lake Travis, and I remember doing a trip to Belize with a friend—also named Maryanne, although she spelled it differently—a serious diver from California. We went to Belize before it was popular, to this amazing little resort owned and operated by a former corporate executive—I think it had less than twenty rooms. Very few other people were there, and it was wonderful.

Although I was now single, I did not date a lot. I met a man in the supermarket, and we went out once, and I had a fling with an executive recruiter I met somewhere along the way. But that was it. I was always very comfortable going out and doing things on my own. I made some friends and felt that I fit in much better in Dallas.

But it is all perspective. Now, looking back, I can tell you that, no, I did not fit in anywhere in Texas. But I certainly fit much better in Dallas, which had much more to offer than Waco. Dallas had people who were from different places and different areas, whereas in Waco, at least at that time, before the couple that renovates houses made it a go-to place, almost everybody was from there, grew up there, stayed there.

Now I had my own nice two-bedroom apartment. I was in a city. I was working as a senior manager for a big firm, and the work was much more interesting and challenging.

I'd gone to work for that firm specifically because I wanted to work with Phil, because I knew him and respected him. But it was not an easy decision. I really liked Mr. J., the partner who interviewed me at another Big Eight firm in Dallas. I'll never forget what he said when I called him and told him I had accepted the job at Phil's firm—because I have used those same words myself many times in the years that followed. He said, "Mary Ann, I understand why you are going where you are. If it does not turn out to be exactly what you expect and want, you always have a job offer here."

I loved working with Phil. Most people did not. I learned this the first day I showed up, when many of my colleagues expressed sentiments along the lines of "Thank God you're here! If the rest of us never have to work with Phil again, it will be fine." Phil was smart, he was demanding, he did not suffer fools, and he would not take people making mistakes lightly. But I learned. Somehow, I intuitively understood that if he was really busy, or if I could sense he did not want to be interrupted for whatever reason, it was not the time to walk into his office to chitchat or ask questions that could wait. But I also knew that with Phil it was all about client service. If there was something I really needed to know and I walked in, even though his original reaction might be visible annoyance, the minute I made the reason I was there clear, he would be helpful and understanding. There was something between us … not something romantic, not in any way, but a connection that made working together and communicating easy.

If I ever had a mentor, it was Phil, but the environment at that firm was less than ideal. The man who ran the tax practice, who I'll call Mr. K., had a reputation for (a) not being a nice guy and (b) being sexist. I was told by a work friend that he'd once made a comment in a meeting where no women were present that if it weren't for the EEOC (Equal Employment Opportunity Commission), he wouldn't have women working there. And this was in 1982 or 1983! Then again, it was also Texas.

One woman at the firm who worked for me, Ms. H., was from Michigan, and over time we became really good friends. We would watch the way Mr. K. would treat our fellow female employee, B., who was senior to me and had spent her entire career at the firm, like almost all the professionals (as I mentioned before, in those days people did not change firms). Mr. K. was absolutely patronizing to this woman. I worked directly with him on a few projects, and he never treated me that way, but he talked to B. like she was a child, saying, "Oh, B., you did such a nice job on that." And B. was totally oblivious. Once day, I forget the context, she turned to Ms. H. and me and said, "I think Mr. K.'s just the greatest." We were floored. One of us, I forget which one, said, "Well, we think he's kind of patronizing."

B.'s response? "I don't even know what that means!"

It was not just Mr. K. The environment in that office at that time was just … odd. One of my first nights at the firm, I went out for drinks with two of my coworkers, and I could tell there was an immediate attraction between me and one of them, D. We spent some time together after that, but then he just completely withdrew, and it never made any sense to me. I could not imagine what I had done. I liked him! Then he ended up literally marrying the new receptionist, who had been a runway model, after dating her for three weeks. Ms. H. and I joked that she showed up at the firm with the wedding dress and everything all picked out—the only thing she did not know was who was going to be the groom.

Many, many years later, D. and I crossed paths and had a drink—and I asked him why he "ran from me." As I remember, his response was that I was "intimidating, smart, and attractive." Which took away a little of the sting.

Sometimes the environment went beyond odd and veered into the toxic. Like when my grandfather died a few months after I started working at the firm. Grandpa had the bad timing to pass away a few days before a tax-filing deadline, and I had to tell Mr. S., the young partner I was working with on one job (male, of course, as there were no female partners at that firm in Dallas in the early 1980s), that we would need to extend the return. I walked into Mr. S.'s office and said, "I'm so sorry. My grandfather died, and I've got to go back to Waco, so we're going to have to extend this client's tax return." And Mr. S. went ballistic.

"Mary Ann, I don't know what you mean!" he yelled. "This company's been a client of this firm forever! Never has their tax return been extended! That is not acceptable! You cannot leave!"

I looked at him in shock and reiterated, "Mr. S., my grandfather died."

He said, "I don't care! I don't care what happened! There's nothing more important than blah, blah, blah …"

I looked at him again. Very calmly I said, "Mr. S., this is the man who raised me. It would be like you losing your father. I have to go back."

And Mr. S. just broke. In an instant, he became a different person. He said, "Oh, Mary Ann, I am so sorry. There's nothing more important than family." He verbally supported my taking the time off, I walked out of his office, and we extended the return.

A few months later, Mr. S. walked to the end of the diving board of his backyard swimming pool, put a gun in his mouth, and blew his brains out.

He had been one of those appear-to-have-it-all people. He was handsome. He was a successful young partner on the fast track. He was seemingly happily married to a beautiful woman.

I remember walking down the hall with Mr. K., and he looked at me and said, "Mary Ann, I suppose you've heard about what happened with Mr. S."

"I did, Mr. K." Then I asked him, "Do we know why?" I was probably trying to find out if there was a note and, if so, what it said.

Mr. K. looked at me. "Well, Mary Ann, we don't know why, but we know it had absolutely nothing to do with this firm."

I walked down the hall thinking, *That is the stupidest thing I ever heard. How could you possibly know that if you didn't know why?* But I kept my somber face.

Later, talking with B., I said, "It's really tragic, but in retrospect there were signs that something was not right." I was thinking back to the way he'd acted when I told him I needed to go to my grandfather's funeral. B. looked at me and said, "Mary Ann, I just don't know why you would say that. He and I were good friends, and I can assure you there was nothing wrong."

I remember thinking, *The man just blew his brains out. What do you mean nothing was wrong?*

I was still seeing Bernie at the time. Once a week, I would drive the ninety or so miles to Waco and the ninety or so miles back, because he was such an important person in my life. I told him the story of what had happened with Mr. S. "This bothers me more than I think it should," I said. "I didn't know him well. I wasn't close to him." I remember that Bernie said, "Mary Ann, don't you know why that bothers you? Had you not gotten out of Waco ... this town was slowly killing you."

That man saved my life. He understood me.

***

One night when my brother, Tommy, was sixteen or seventeen, he showed up at my apartment in Dallas. He told me he had run away from home. I told my brother I loved him, but I also remember saying, "But you didn't even call me" and "What if I hadn't been home?" I assume we called Dorothy and Daddy. I probably called and said, "He's here, he's safe, and he'll stay here tonight."

Obviously, he was dealing with some issues—I do not remember whether they told me before or after he ran away, but I remember Daddy and Dorothy telling me that he was depressed, and once they talked about him hiding under the car.

I was so worried that I asked Bernie what to do. "Bernie, Tommy seems to be going through something. What do I do, and what can happen? Should I be worried? Would he hurt himself? Would he commit suicide?"

Of course, the answer was the simplest thing in the world. "Ask him," Bernie said. "Because most people, if they are suicidal, will tell you."

I have some very specific memories, but so much of it is just a blur. It is as if I moved on and filed it away somewhere … or didn't.

***

After about two years at my job, I remember deciding, *This place isn't for me. I need to move on.* I called Mr. J., the tax partner in charge at the other firm who had interviewed me and offered me a position when I first moved to Dallas. I said, "Mr. J., I don't know if you remember me."

"Of course I remember," he said.

"Well, you once told me if everything didn't work out, your door was always open. If that offer is still open, I'd like to come interview. Would you consider taking me?"

The hardest part was telling Phil I was leaving. He said, "Mary Ann, I get it. I'm sorry you're going." He actually didn't stay that long at the firm either. Sometime after I left, he went to work for one of his clients. That tells you something. Phil had changed firms three times, which was not common with partners, and he was a senior, successful partner. When he left, it made me feel that *I'm not crazy. There's something going on there.*

Before I started at my new firm, I took a vacation to Cancún. I went with Maryanne and met a man who was there with his married friends. He and I had a magical, if brief, affair. But alas, he was married, and although we met once after that, he broke it off to save his marriage.

I, meanwhile, started my new job. And it was different.

At this point in my career, I had risen to the level of being one promotion away from partner. That did not mean I would be reaching that milestone in a matter of months—making partner doesn't happen quickly. You spend a long time as a manager or senior manager, "running the client" and keeping them happy and training and developing the people under you. But honestly, the way to get admitted to the partnership at a Big Eight firm is to help that firm grow, and the way you grow is by bringing in new business. So there is networking and making substantive business contacts and relationships, and you also have to be really, really good at what you do. After all, accounting, auditing, and consulting is, at its core, a technical business.

I was good at figuring out how to be helpful to my clients and also at knowing the firm's resources and understanding how to effectively marshal those resources to deliver outstanding client service. And I knew the value of building relationships with partners throughout the firm. I especially enjoyed working with the expert resources in the Washington, DC, office—one of the partners there once told me, "When you call, your message always goes to the top of the stack."

I was surprised. To be honest, I'd never thought about a top or a bottom of the stack. I asked, "Really?" and they said, "You don't think we return everybody's calls as quickly as we do yours, do you?"

"What? I hadn't thought about it."

And they said, "And the reason is because when you call, you're prepared and efficient, and you often have the answer and only need confirmation." I knew it was not just me; obviously I was working with a team of dedicated, talented people who were also responsible. But they were *my* team.

Was it my dream job, the one I thought and wrote about when I was a girl, like being a doctor or astronaut? Of course not. But I enjoyed it. I enjoyed strategizing, spending time with my clients and delivering outstanding client service, engaging with prospective clients, and seeing how much I, a motherless girl from Mart, could accomplish.

My one real issue was the fact that some partners at my new firm in Dallas did not like me. I am saying this with a retrospective view, and it may sound harsh—part of it was that these partners were sexist. But part of it was just me. That part of me that, no matter where I went, did not seem to fit in.

For example, I have always loved clothes, and as I climbed the corporate ladder, my fashion budget continued to expand. I had started shopping in the couture department at Neiman Marcus but according to my budget—meaning I might be able to buy one or two outfits, and I almost always bought on sale. To be honest, I still do.

I bought the most incredible suit—a solid burgundy jacket trimmed with olive-green velvet, combined with this gorgeous, midcalf pleated skirt with very subtle burgundy and green flowers on it and a wide olive-green belt that matched the trim on the jacket. I do not remember the designer, but it was one of my favorite outfits— certainly not a "turn a man's pant into a skirt" kind of suit. I wore it to work one day, and one of the partners approached me and asked, "How many colors are in that skirt?" Another day I came in wearing a beautiful red suit. Another partner looked me up and down with some distaste and then said, "You know, Mary Ann, you could go to Brooks Brothers and find a suit like mine."

Despite that, I rose in the ranks. I was included on the teams they sent to review other offices, which is something you don't get to do unless you are competent and doing well. Which I was.

***

One day, my friend and sometimes lover from the Hong Kong flight called me—not because he was going to be in Dallas but with a business prospect. "I've got this friend," he explained. "He just sold out of a company. He's bored. He's looking for something to do. Do you ever come across companies for sale?" My friend explained that while he was at Harvard Business School, this man was working for a prominent consulting firm in Boston.

Being the good practice-development person I was, I said, "Sure, give him my name." While I was sitting at my desk one day, the phone rang, and when I answered, the voice on the other end introduced himself as the man my friend had told me about. He told me a little about what he was looking for, and we agreed to meet and discuss it further over lunch.

I belonged to a luncheon club in Dallas and arranged to meet him there. I remember waiting, and while I was waiting, this man got off the elevator. It was as if a thunderbolt hit me. The very first thought in my mind was *Oh, my God, there's the man I'm going to marry.*

It turned out he was also the man I was having lunch with!

My lunch date was Cary Grant handsome. He was athletic enough to have played semiprofessional soccer, with a classic face and an athletic, Greek body—six feet tall, 175 pounds, and in great shape, although some of this became clearer later. I was still a dedicated practice-development person and took all the notes and did all the things I was supposed to do … although as my new prospective client always said, *What business luncheon lasts three hours?*

In retrospect, it was love at first sight for me, although I did not know or acknowledge it then.

The next morning, I had set up a meeting with the partner to whom I was going to introduce the new prospective client, to brief him ahead of time. I explained who the man was, that he had three degrees—after he got his degree in Shakespearean literature, which meant he was doing nothing, he went back to a university on the West Coast and earned a degree in geological oceanography and then came back to Texas for his MBA. I told him where he had worked and what company he had sold out of and all the relevant information.

This partner looked at me and said, "Mary Ann, this man isn't ever going to be a client. This is some guy you're going to fall in love with and marry."

I always liked being single. I wasn't looking. I certainly was not looking to get married.

We had the meeting, and Mr. Cary Grant Handsome did not end up working with my firm. He asked me out. I purchased tickets to an Alfred Brendel concert. The intensity of our chemistry became clear that evening.

Or course, in retrospect, that may be because he was a sex addict. I still do not know.

***

Mr. Cary Grant Handsome and I became a couple almost immediately. The chemistry was incredible. The first night we made love, he told me he loved me.

But at the same time, he would go away for days or weeks, and I would not see him and he would not call. This was long before texting, so it was as if he basically disappeared. I did not understand. He always had an explanation. I will never know if they were true or not.

He was also insanely jealous. One night he came over, and my former coworker D., who had married the model/receptionist, had left a message on my answering machine saying he needed to talk to me. The model/receptionist had left him. He was a friend, so I called, and we talked. And my new boyfriend was really upset. I had to convince him that "There's nothing there."

Still, he was different from any man I had ever been with before. He introduced me to a whole new world. One night, he called after I had gone to bed. He had been to a party to which I had not been invited and was calling to ask me out for a late-night after-party date. I got up, put on makeup, did my hair, and chose a cocktail dress from my closet. It was a beautiful silk fabric with large, abstract flowers in shades of black and gray, a skirt that flowed, and long sleeves that did the same, with a sash that I tied in a bow at the waist. He showed up in his perfectly fitted tux. We went to the Venetian Room at the Fairmont Hotel, had cocktails, and watched a show—my memory is that it was Tony Bennett, but I do not know for certain. After it was over, when we were leaving the hotel, we stepped into an elevator and another couple followed us in. The woman looked at us and said, "I'm sorry, and forgive me for staring at you and saying this, but you two are just the most gorgeous couple." I'm sure we looked happy. I know I was.

My new boyfriend and I both loved adventure and the water. He was an accomplished boatsman and had a twenty-two-foot Boston Whaler that we would take to Lake Texoma and go exploring. His second degree was in geological oceanography, so we would hunt for rocks and fossils. Once we found a nautilus fossil—it may have even been on our first excursion there together. I brought that nautilus home, and it followed me everywhere for many years.

Another time we trailered the boat from Dallas to Fort Lauderdale, launched in Fort Lauderdale, and went island hopping in the Bahamas for two weeks. It was an incredible trip and a great adventure. The first stop after Fort Lauderdale was Bimini, and when we arrived, the first thing we saw was the boat *Monkey Business*, where Senator Gary Hart's presidential dreams were shattered. We sailed from Bimini to Cat Cay, Cat Cay to Chub Cay, and finally to the Exumas. It was incredibly romantic. Being in that twenty-two-foot Whaler, we were so close to the water. One morning as we were motoring around, I remember my boyfriend telling me to look down, and there on the starboard side of the boat, in this spectacularly clear-blue Atlantic water, barely below the surface I saw this magnificent creature, longer than our boat. It was a whale shark. Before seeing one, I had not known this imposing creature existed. I now know this gentle giant is the largest living fish, a filter feeder that neither bites nor chews. Some nights we would even camp out on the boat. It was magical.

Somewhere along the way to the Exumas, we came across what was clearly a drug operation. We encountered a large fishing boat cruising with fishing poles mounted on the stern, lines in the water. It pulled up beside us, and several shady-looking men with shirts unbuttoned almost to their waists and gold chains asked, "Where are you guys going?" I remember my boyfriend said, "We're looking to get to Chub Cay. Are we on the right track?" They said we were and told us to keep going.

Then they turned around and took off, and we noticed multiple huge motors as we also took off full throttle toward Chub Cay. Our boat took such a pounding that there was damage to some of the instruments and equipment.

We knew we had witnessed one party to an illegal transaction of some type.

When we got to the Exumas, we rented a cottage on one of the small cays. One morning at breakfast we met a couple who had this beautiful fifty-foot ketch moored in the harbor. We became vacation friends and met their nephews who were with them. They or their nephews would go out fishing with us in the Whaler, and for dinner, in their galley, they would cook the catch of the day.

One night another couple they knew, also moored in the harbor, joined our group for drinks and dinner. They said, "We saw the strangest thing one night. We were in Chub Cay, and we saw this little boat that was tied up to the dock. And honestly we thought it was somebody's tender. But when we looked closer, we think there was somebody that was literally traveling in that boat."

My boyfriend and I looked at each other and then looked at them and said, "That would be us." They suggested we should write our story up for a travel magazine, because navigating the Bahamas in such a small boat was not for the faint of heart.

Another night after dinner we were going back to our cabin, going in slowly because we were where everybody was moored, and all of a sudden lights came on and this other boat took off like the proverbial bat out of hell. We just knew. *We have come across another drug operation.* It was quite an adventure. And it was gorgeous, to be able to explore in that part of the world. We could just pull up on a beach in the boat. We scuba dived in the same cave where they filmed the James Bond movie *Thunderball.*

That was our first trip together.

As we got more serious, I pressed my boyfriend to introduce me to his family. I met his mother over lunch at Dallas Country Club, described as follows in Wikipedia: "The club, according to the *Dallas*

Morning News, has been a staple of Highland Park's most exclusive social circuit for more than a century." It also notes that "the club did not admit its first African American member until 2014, after a 13-year application process." My boyfriend's family were longtime members of the club and in the *Social Register*, but his mother was more than just another society widow. She had been the first woman to graduate from SMU law school, at the age of twenty-one, and had gone back to school for her master's in international law when my boyfriend and his brother were teenagers. She told me her dream was to join the OAS (Organization of American States) and that she had actually been invited but chose to turn it down when, at a dinner party, she heard someone say to her husband, "How's it going to feel to be Mr. Missus?" She told me, "When I heard that, I couldn't do that to him." She was also incredibly beautiful. Naturally. She was beautiful in the pictures of her as a young woman, had aged gracefully, without plastic surgery or Botox, and was still beautiful in her seventies and eighties, and even in her nineties.

I characterize my boyfriend's relationship with his mother as a little creepy. She always referred to him as "darling" or "honey," and if we were in a car, she would sit in the front seat with him, and I would be relegated to the back seat. It wasn't sexual, but it felt … inappropriate. As I look back, it was an obvious red flag. But I was head over heels in love.

It did not help matters that my boyfriend's mother did not like me. I knew this because I did a bad thing. There were so many unanswered questions. I could never completely trust him, and my emotions were always running high, so one day, on impulse, I went through his briefcase. I found letters to him from his mother, and I read them. She went to great and eloquent lengths, listing for her son everything that was wrong with me. He could find someone prettier, someone from a better family, someone who was smarter, someone who wasn't divorced …

She was also divorced, but nobody talked about that. My boyfriend's father was a widower with a toddler, my boyfriend's half brother. No one talked about how they'd met or how long they dated, but they were married in February 1942, and he was immediately shipped overseas to the European theater, leaving her to raise this young boy for two years. My boyfriend was born in September of 1945. A classic war baby.

***

In 1986, a few months after our relationship started, the financial crisis hit the savings and loan industry and much of Texas. My firm was undertaking staff reductions, and my name was on the list. I do not know the details, but I imagine a partners' meeting taking place to discuss the situation and two or three of those partners very quickly putting my name on the list.

Again, I do not know any of that for sure. But I remember Mr. J., who had been a fan of mine from the beginning, saying, "Mary Ann, this just isn't going to work here."

It was not one of those "You're out the door tomorrow" situations. It was more "We're giving you a chance to go on and do something different … pursue other interests." If I had a family and a husband to support me, they might have said, "Spend time with your family." What it meant to me was *Oh shit, I've got to find a job.*

I remembered meeting the partner who ran the LA office when I was part of the review team. I called him up and said, "It's not going to work for me in Dallas. And now's a good time for me to think about leaving. I think maybe I'd like to move out to LA. Would you help me?"

"Mary Ann," he said, "I'll get you some interviews out here …
but I'd love to have you here."

"Seriously?" I said.

I made arrangements to go interview in California.

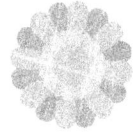

CHAPTER 3

LOS ANGELES

My boyfriend accompanied me to LA for my interviews, and I was offered the job at the firm's Los Angeles office. Afterward, back in Dallas, we had lunch and talked about the prospect of my leaving Texas for the West Coast. "Mary Ann," he said, "of course you've got to take it. It's the only job we've got between the two of us, and we'll just see what happens."

So I took the job. I went out to LA, found an apartment, and moved. And within a month or two or three, my boyfriend also found a job in LA—well, in Orange County, which is one county south of Los Angeles County. So he had an apartment in Orange County, I had an apartment in LA, and I stayed with him, mostly, and did the drive north to work every morning. Why? Because I was in love with him and did stupid things I would never do today.

And there were still those red flags. My boyfriend came from money, and he spent money, but he did not always *have* money. At one point he borrowed $15,000 from me—I forget the exact reason. I remember, however, that a screaming fight and ultimatum had to transpire in order for me to be repaid. We also fought about his mother, whom he helped support in the style to which she had long been accustomed. I would say, "Wait a minute—you are sending a check to your mother every month, and she drives a better car than I do. Can you explain? I have a problem with this."

But mostly we fought about getting married—specifically, about the fact that I wanted to make our partnership official and he did not. At one point he kicked me out of his apartment without telling me he was going to do so. To be specific, he took everything I had at his place in Orange County and moved it to my place in LA. I found out only after it was a done deal. After that I rarely, if ever, went back to his apartment, and then he started staying with me. At least it meant I didn't have to drive in traffic, which in LA can be extremely helpful.

In retrospect, I realized a lot of our fighting was because it was always about him and what he wanted. At the time, I did not know what was wrong, only that something *felt* wrong, and I could never get to the place where I felt it was right. We both agreed we needed help with our communication and booked an appointment with a therapist ... actually, multiple therapists. The first had us take the Myers-Briggs personality test, which pointed out the differences in our communication styles, and my boyfriend latched on to it. We were both big *Star Trek* fans and science-fiction lovers, so suddenly I was the "irrational" one—the emotional, volatile Captain Kirk to his cool, logical Mr. Spock.

I remember getting an overall feeling that this therapist was not listening to me and only listened to what my boyfriend had to say. What I now realize is that my boyfriend manipulated him. I watched how he worked the therapist and turned me into "the problem." "Here are all the things that are wrong with her," and "She's got anger issues," and blah-blah-blah. At one appointment, I had the audacity to express my feelings about the dynamic among the three of us, although I have no memory of exactly what I said. What I do remember is the therapist's instant, dramatic reaction to my words. They must have hit too close to home, because he became so angry he was physically shaking. I got up and said, "I'm done," and I left.

We found another psychologist in Santa Monica. His name was Bob, and he was really, really good. He coached us on communication and how we needed to talk to each other. It must have gone well, because at some point along the way we adopted two cats, whom we named Sherman and Patton, and started taking them into therapy with us. Bob would say, "These cats have been good for you guys." There were a lot of good times, at least in the beginning.

As for my parental instincts, being a cat mom was as far as that was going to go. I knew that I did not want to have children, and if we were going to be together forever, I needed to make sure my boyfriend was okay with that. He had never had children and was already in his forties, and if he had his heart set on becoming a father, that might have been a deal-breaker for me. So I asked, and he was agnostic about the whole thing. I think he would have been okay having children if I'd wanted them, but he personally did not care. I had my tubes tied and never considered asking him to have a vasectomy. He may not have wanted children then, but if something happened to me and he married someone else, he might have changed his mind.

By 1988, we had been dating for three years and there was still no ring on my finger. And I gave him an ultimatum. I was serious, and he knew I was serious. I had worked it out with Bob, our therapist. I put a deadline on it. *This is it. And after that day, we're done. Period.*

And it worked.

I vividly remember my boyfriend proposing to me, at dinner in a very nice LA restaurant, for two reasons. Number one, because it had taken so much to get there, and number two, because after all that, he gave me his grandmother's engagement ring. It was a beautiful heirloom piece. You do not give heirloom jewelry to just anybody, certainly not in his family. That meant something, and it was reassuring.

It meant something to my future mother-in-law as well. The minute we were engaged, she embraced me. I remember my now-fiancé had always said, "It'll be fine," and he was right. She even started letting me call her by her first name. However, I still had to live with the baggage caused by her years of malign writings as well as the coldness she often displayed toward me throughout my marriage to her son. Knowing firsthand the harm this can cause, I often quote a friend who once told me, "Mary Ann, I treat every woman either of my sons dates as if she could be my daughter-in-law." Very wise words.

***

Getting my boyfriend to propose did not mean I suddenly started getting everything I wanted from him. During our engagement, I got something I very much did not want—a new boat. He had his eye on a thirty-six-foot Sea Ray powerboat, and while we both loved boats and the water, I did not want him to buy it. It was expensive, the maintenance would be expensive … everything about it was expensive. I told him I thought we needed to be a bit more frugal.

He came home one day and told me, "I bought the boat."

I don't remember the original name of the boat, but he changed it to *Adventurous II*, after the beloved little Boston Whaler, which was named *Adventurous*. Apparently changing a boat's name is bad luck, and this boat brought me plenty of it. The original *Adventurous* and I had great karma. My fiancé always had a great time when he went out on his new boat without me. But almost every time I got on

Adventurous II, something went wrong. Once, we took it out with a group of people who worked for him, and one of them, while trying to help dock the boat in our slip next to the seawall, let it crash into the rocks. That was just one instance of many, although I can't remember all the specifics. I just remember knowing that the name change was not the only reason that boat and I had bad karma.

***

Once we were finally engaged, it was time for me to meet the rest of the family, who lived on the East Coast. We met his uncle, his mother's older brother, who was loved and admired by everyone in the family, and his wife. I was told by my future mother-in-law that the uncle's wife was "old East Coast" and did not know how to boil water because she'd grown up with servants to attend to her every need. Their three sons and their families were there, as was my fiancé's brother and his wife.

His uncle hosted an engagement party at a club in Stamford, Connecticut. I remember him toasting me by saying, "We all owe my nephew gratitude for bringing Mary Ann to this family." That was how he treated me from the first moment and for the rest of his life. His oldest son and wife hosted a pool party for us at their exquisite Greenwich, Connecticut, estate, and everyone from out of town stayed at a charming inn. Since this trip was to celebrate our engagement, my future mother-in-law said, "Mary Ann, you should have the suite." It had a sitting room and a bedroom.

Of course, my fiancé slept with me, but we could never admit it to his mother because it would have been inappropriate to have sex before marriage. She stopped by at some point, walked into the sitting room, and noticed magazines spread everywhere. She looked at me and said, "Oh, I see my son has been here."

Being surrounded by all these people of wealth and breeding, who had never known anything else, was a very different world for this girl from Mart, Texas, to find herself in. I do not know exactly where the self-confidence to be a part of this world came from.

Despite the difference in our backgrounds, my fiancé was very good and kind toward my dad, Dorothy, and Tommy. My dad never told me what he thought of my fiancé, but they were always welcoming to him. And while, when I divorced husband #1, my father had told me that if I ever got married again, he would not be there, he did, in fact, come to my second wedding. But I did not want him to walk me down the aisle. I was having none of that. I was a grown woman.

It was a small wedding at a Congregational Church somewhere in Orange County, followed by a reception at the Balboa Bay Club in Newport Beach. We were married by one of the partners from my firm who was an ordained minister, at ten o'clock in the morning in front of approximately fifty people. It was November 19, the day that UCLA and USC were playing their annual football game, so some guests periodically excused themselves to the bar area to keep an eye on what I now know is a very important event.

I didn't wear a white dress. I was a bit unsettled and jittery about the whole thing. And my soon-to-be mother-in-law was very intrusive. In the months and weeks before the wedding she sent me letters observing that "Nobody gets married at ten o'clock in the morning" and offering other pieces of (unwanted) advice. She was intrusive right up to my wedding day, hovering in the area where I was dressing. I finally asked a friend to please find my fiancé and get him to take her away.

But it was a beautiful wedding on a picture-perfect Southern California November day. Late that afternoon we took family and friends out on *Adventurous II*. The water was calm, and we had cocktails and watched the sea lions play. Even my bad boat karma did not make an appearance.

That night there was an earthquake. Looking back, maybe I should have regarded it as a sign. An even bigger sign appeared the next morning, when my new husband got up early and left our marital bed to go take his mother for a boat ride.

Then, on the way back to LA from Orange County, my bad boat karma made its appearance. *Adventurous II* lost a propeller and literally had to be towed into the harbor. That is when my husband #2 announced that he had invited his mother to dinner the next night.

"Seriously?" I said.

I had no idea what I had gotten myself into.

My dad and Dorothy had a wonderful time. They had never traveled much, and coming to California and staying at the Balboa Bay Club in a room looking out on the harbor was a cherished experience. Afterward, they flew up to San Francisco. I remember Dorothy telling me, "We just had the most wonderful trip. In the mornings we would have coffee in our room, looking at the water."

I told my husband about the fabulous little resort where I had dived in Belize, on St. George's Caye. We went there for our honeymoon, and when we arrived, the group I used to dive with in Dallas happened to be there. It was totally coincidental and a great surprise. The way #2 would tell the story, we walked in for our honeymoon, and there were all these guys coming up and hugging his wife, saying, "Oh, so nice to see you! Mary Ann, what are you doing here?" It was hysterical.

The place was quite remote at that time, and the only other thing I remember being on the caye was a British R & R station. The diving was unspoiled and spectacular. There were so few other people you could count them on your hands. The mosquitoes were horrible.

Overall, the experience was charming and romantic. The last night we were there, only one or two other couples remained—my former diving group had left very soon after we arrived. We all ate together at a small rectangular table, and the kitchen made us a special cake that read, "Congratulations, M and M." Fred, the resort's owner, opened up two bottles of Dom Pérignon to celebrate the evening.

It was a beautiful beginning.

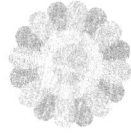

CHAPTER 4

JUST MARRIED

In later years, after things had taken a dark turn, #2 characterized our marriage this way: the first ten years were great, the next five, not so great, and the last five, horrible. Those first ten years I was madly in love with him, and it seemed that he was with me. It wasn't perfect. There were the fights over his mother, his boat, and the usual couple things. But it was very much a marriage, and we were very much working together as a team. We enjoyed a lot of the same things, including science, learning, and travel. He was a smart, interesting, sexy man, and I loved being married to him.

He was nine years older than I and had led a full life before he met me. He had dated the beauty queens, debutantes, and society girls you would expect a handsome Dallas Country Club *Social Register* man to date. I would tell him, "I'm glad you did all that. I'm glad that you experimented." Whatever that was, I was happy he had gotten it out of his system.

When we first married, we continued to live in the small two-story townhouse on Olympic Boulevard that I'd first rented when I moved from Dallas to LA. Before we married, #2 had been staying with me and "our" cats, Sherman and Patton, most if not all of the time. Once we were married and he gave up his apartment, there was the matter of all his stuff. He had inherited a lot of furniture from his grandmother that he had kept in storage for many years when he was working and traveling, never bothering to move it into his apartment in Orange County. But now that he was a married man, he had all his worldly possessions delivered to his new home, which was, I remind you, a small two-bedroom, one-and-a-half-bathroom townhouse that we were sharing with two cats. There was stuff everywhere. It quickly became an issue, neither of us wanting to give up our things. Finally a friend came over to act as referee. "Okay, she gives up something; now you have to give up something." It was almost overwhelming.

We eventually hired a professional interior designer to help us turn my little apartment into our home. We worked with an older woman and her husband who had been designers to the rich and famous, and they came with great stories. They helped us redo that little place so that it was quite lovely, though still quite small for two cats and two people who loved to entertain. The four of us shared a bathroom! But we lived there many years, and for most of those years we were that loving couple, always holding hands, having fun together. I felt like we were the perfect team.

***

In 1988, I was put up for partner at my firm. No legions of female partners existed in any accounting, professional services, or law firm, nor in the senior executive ranks in any industry, so this was still a rarity. However, I would not be the first in my firm.

In order to become a partner, I had to be voted in by all the partners—not just the partners with whom I worked in the LA office who had submitted me but partners representing the whole of the company on what was called the Firm Council, which was the governing body, similar to a board of directors. In reality, the Firm Council represented the real power players in the firm. As part of the assessment and review process, they would review your file and talk with any and all partners of their choosing. That meant that people from the Dallas office, where I had effectively been let go, were going to have a say in my future. The process was secretive, so I had no idea what anyone said about me. And while I do not know it to be true, the perception at that time was that any one partner could derail you.

I did not make it. I was what they referred to as "deferred." I do not remember what they said or why, and I knew some of it was also a numbers game. There had to be a need for a new partner to add a new partner. But I have no doubt that baggage from Dallas came up when they were considering me.

At the same time, a man whom I worked with in LA was also up for partner. It was well known that this man was an alcoholic. Sometime during that year, in the conference room on the top floor of the building, he had a fight with a coworker and literally punched him. He committed violence at work in the workplace. This was a well-known fact. He made partner; I did not.

Many years later, this man left the firm. I am not sure if it was voluntarily or if he was forced out. He went to work for a large public company on the East Coast and was caught up in a high-profile corporate scandal. I believe he went to prison.

The following year I was again put up for partner and once again was deferred. The writing appeared to be on the wall. Common sense, as well as the personal advice of more than one partner, told me that nobody could be deferred twice and go on to make partner. It was simply not possible. I knew that the people who knew me best, the people who worked with me on a daily basis, the clients, the partners, my colleagues, all supported me. But clearly that was not enough.

You know what? I reasoned. *I have got baggage here I will never get over. There's only so much I can do.* In my mind, I had gone as far as I was ever going to go at this firm. I discreetly found a position at another top firm that promised me the opportunity for a relatively near-term path to partner. Then I turned in my resignation.

Mr. S., the partner who had first brought me to LA, called me into his office after he read my resignation letter. "I understand why you're doing this," he said. "I accept it." But he also asked me to meet with the managing partner who ran the office before I made a final decision. Ultimately, he set it up for me to talk to not just the person running the greater LA area but also one of the vice chairmen in the firm.

I sat down with the vice chairman, and he asked me, "Why are you leaving?"

I had been grilled by this man before—during my partner interviews. He was notorious for being smart, no nonsense, demanding, and a bit of a jerk. During one of my previous rounds, which ultimately resulted in my being deferred, he looked at me and said, "Mary Ann, you're married. If I make you a partner, what if I need you to move?" I had told him, "My husband and I know we are a two-career family. We will deal with it." But clearly that had not been enough.

"Well," I reminded him, "you know everything about me. I've been deferred twice. I've had any number of partners tell me that there's no such thing as being deferred twice, and I'll never be a partner here."

He looked at me and said, "Mary Ann, first off, that's not right."

It wasn't?

"I think we have a lot of partners here who don't have the courage to tell people the unvarnished truth," he explained. "So we have a lot of

JUST MARRIED | 55

people who never should be put in the partner process, and rather than somebody telling them, 'Oh, you're never going to be a partner here because you don't have everything it takes,' they use the word *deferred*."

Which is exactly what I assumed had been happening to me.

But then he said, "That is not your case. I am telling you, you will be a partner in this firm. And not only do I think you will be a partner in this firm; I think you'll be a great partner in this firm."

I stayed. I made partner the next year.

On the other hand, one of the partners in Dallas (all men) who I know did not like me, who may have been in no small part responsible for those deferrals, was fired from the firm. The others never went on to be on the board or serve on any high-profile committees like I did. I went on to have what most would consider a significantly more successful career. I guess, in Los Angeles, I finally found a place where I fit in. Or at least where I fit in better.

At one of my first firm-wide partner meetings, I saw one of the partners from Dallas. He had played college football at one of the then Southwest Conference universities and absolutely did not know how to relate to me—or maybe to anyone. He spotted me, and it was almost like he plastered himself against the wall on the other side of the room just so he would not have to come over and say hello. It was pretty funny.

Throughout my life, I have almost always looked for the silver lining in my inevitable difficult experiences. And later, whenever I was the partner who had to counsel somebody who experienced the disappointment of being up for partner and not making it, I always felt that in its own bizarre way, I had been given that gift of being able to say, "I know exactly what you're going through." I could offer more than just words. I could actually say, "I've been there, and I know how much it hurts." Because it does hurt. It's rejection. But I am living proof it doesn't have to be the end.

I still feel uncomfortable sharing anything that is or could appear to be tooting my own horn. I truly believe that mostly I just worked hard and tried to do the best I could for my clients and the firm. But I have to admit that I was good at what I did, or I would never have achieved what I did. I brought a strong work ethic and passion to client service and all the other roles I had in the firm. That is part of what made me a good partner. It was a drive and determination to do whatever I had to do to get it done. Whether it was working on a client or firm project, spending time to counsel or train staff, or recruiting, if I was going to do it, I gave it my all.

I also had another quality that served me well at this phase of my life and career, and it still does—knowing what I do and do not know and asking for help. In those early years, my husband was a really good business coach. He was older and had more savvy and experience, so he was a great sounding board for me. I remember at one point, even after I was a partner, feeling very much like the odd duck in my organization, wondering if I should be doing something different. Maybe I should get a job with a client. My husband was able to explain exactly why that would not work for me. "Mary Ann, you would be miserable in industry," he said. "You are in an organization where you essentially are on the front lines. You're the revenue-generating part of the organization. If you ever went into industry, you would be in a staff position." He was absolutely right. I would be "the finance person" or "tax person" or "accounting person." At my firm, I was the product.

He also asked me, and it served me well over the years, "What do you most enjoy about what you do?"

I thought about it, and when I was really honest with myself, I realized it was the pursuit and winning of new clients and new projects. It was developing and executing the strategy to get a new client, win a big project, hire the best people, or get the very best from everyone who reported to me. You might not get that just by looking at me. I am not very tall, and I am not very loud, and I may come off like a sweet little lady who grew up somewhere in the South. But underneath this nonthreatening demeanor is a very nice, very polite tigress.

***

Eventually, money tensions started to creep into the marriage. My husband was working, but he was not making as much money as I was. And he was spending more money than I could ever have imagined. Everything he made went to keeping *Adventurous II* docked, maintained, and operating and, together with his brother, supporting their mother, who continued to live in the high style to which she was accustomed. "We are living in a little townhouse," I reminded him. "You are sending money to your mother every month. She lives in a much nicer place than I do. She *still* drives a much nicer car than I do. What is wrong with this picture?"

As I would soon learn, a lot more than I'd ever imagined.

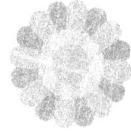

CHAPTER 5

BIG FISH, BIG POND

I made partner in 1990, and in 1998 the firm merged with another Big Six accounting firm to become PricewaterhouseCoopers LLP, known as PwC. I remember the day we received the news, thinking, *Wow, okay, I'm going to live through a merger.* I also thought it would be great for both firms. I went into it with the attitude of *You know what? All these people I didn't know yesterday are going to be my partners and colleagues as soon as this deal closes.* I had a completely open mind and an optimistic attitude and mindset. That probably served me very well, because I was generally accepted by both sides, and many were not.

Many or maybe even most people view a merger as a threat and approach it with an us-versus-them mentality. My attitude and approach were the opposite of that, and I quickly gained the trust and support of the partners I met and worked with from the other side of the merger. A few years later, I made the short list for consideration for the board of partners. I was not elected, but not long afterward I was asked to serve on a committee to choose the US firm's new CEO.

Both these events had a significant impact on my career, enhancing my profile within the firm and further elevating my professional and career experience. Plus, I met J., who became a great friend as well as partner. J. had also been short-listed but not elected to the board. Because we had been fully vetted through that process and had the trust and respect of our partners, we were both logical choices for the CEO selection committee.

When you are nominated to the board of partners at PwC, it is truly a milestone. Every partner in the firm can and is encouraged to talk with the selection committee, which is why I (and probably any partner who has been through the process or served on the committee) believe that the people who vet you for the board of partners know more about you than you know about yourself. The partners they talk with can and do share all the "bad things" about you in addition to the good. The process is completely confidential and respectful, concluding when the committee sorts through all the information and determines if you have the attributes and qualifications to serve on the board.

When I was eventually elected to the board, I was both humbled and honored. The election process is one partner, one vote, with the same ranking and selection process that is used for choosing the Academy Award winners. To have been elected to both the US and global boards … I still can hardly believe it happened to me.

I had the privilege of doing many different things throughout my career. It opened many doors and enabled me to see much of the world in a special and privileged way. I also met and worked with incredible and accomplished people. My boss back in Waco had warned me about being a little fish in a big pond when I could have stayed in Waco and been a big fish in a little pond. I don't think anyone expected I would somehow end up being a big fish in a giant pond. Least of all me.

One day as I was standing in my office on the fiftieth floor, looking at the Los Angeles view I had from my windows, I was suddenly overcome with the feeling that I needed to talk to Phil. He was the person who'd started me on my path right out of Baylor, when he offered me that position in Houston that I did not take because I was married. Phil was the person who'd helped me get into that national firm in Waco and, after I divorced, make the move to Dallas. I remembered he had left the firm where we had both worked and gone on and done other things, and I had heard he was in Dallas working part time for another firm, now part of the Big Five. So I called their Dallas office and asked the receptionist if Phil worked there. She said he did and put my call through, and then Phil was on the line. That is how easy it was.

"I think of you so often," I told him. "Back when you and I worked together, people didn't talk about mentors. But if I ever had anybody in my career who was a mentor, it is you. I am grateful for everything you did for me, whether or not you even knew you did it. And I just wanted to tell you what's happened with me in my career. I will always be so grateful to you for all you did for me—the doors you opened for me to walk through, the training from actually working for you, and most of all for encouraging me."

I told Phil how far I had come in my career. "That's fabulous to hear." Then he said, "It's interesting you should call. I was just diagnosed with esophageal cancer. I'm having surgery next week. It's a tough surgery, but there's every reason to believe this can be treated."

I told him how sorry I was that he was going through this and that I hoped it would all be okay, and we ended the call.

Around two weeks later, I was standing at my desk in my LA office and the phone rang. I answered as I always did, saying "Mary Ann Cloyd." A woman who had worked at the same firm in Dallas in the early 1980s (the one I joined because of Phil) had tracked me down. "Mary Ann," she said, "I don't know if you remember me, and I wasn't sure how to find you." I told her I remembered her well. Then she said, "I wanted to let you know Phil passed away."

I don't know what had possessed me to pick up the phone that day and call my friend and former boss, to thank him and let him know how much he meant to me and how important a role he had played in my life. But I am awfully glad I did.

***

I am a cautious spender, maybe because I do not come from much. So my husband and I stayed in our small, rented townhouse on Olympic Boulevard for years and years. One night, we had a dinner party for our interior designer, her husband, the woman who first introduced us to them, C., and C.'s husband, D. I love to cook and entertain, but our kitchen and dining area were both small. If one person wanted to leave the table, others had to get up and move to make room for them to do so.

D. was asthmatic and allergic to cats, so we kept Sherman and Patton in the bedroom upstairs and away from our guests. But in that tiny apartment, where the cats, when guests were not present, were free to go wherever they wanted, including on the furniture, that was not enough of an escape. We had just finished the meal and I was about to bring out dessert when D. looked at C. and said, "You stay and have coffee. I'm reacting to the cats. I'm going to go to the car."

My husband had asthma, too, so he was familiar with what D. was experiencing. After dessert, when everyone was saying goodbye, he suggested I go to the car with C. and bring D. a glass of water. We walked over—the car was only a block away—but C. insisted I get in the front seat with D. and they would drive me the block back home. So I got in the front seat. C. got in the back seat and closed the door. And the next thing I saw was a face at the window pulling the door open with a gun at D.'s head and another guy behind him.

He yelled, "Give us what you've got."

I was wearing a beautiful diamond-and-yellow-gold necklace my husband had given me for our anniversary. The guy literally ripped the necklace off my neck. He looked at us and said, "If you don't give us everything you've got, we will kill you."

I wasn't wearing my engagement ring, only my simple gold wedding band. I pulled it off and said, "This is all." I pushed the sleeves of my sweater up to show them my bare arms. "I have nothing else."

D. got out his wallet and gave one of them money. Meanwhile, C. threw her ring on the floor of the car, somehow got out of the car, and ran into the street screaming. Then D. threw the water in his glass over my head and right into the face of one of the robbers. That caused a commotion, and I was able to get out of the car and call for my husband to help us. He came running down the street. I yelled, "We've been robbed!"

The two men ran off just as my husband reached us. C. was still in the street, still screaming. I do not know who called 911, but the police showed up and questioned each one of us separately. The police officer talking to me spotted the water spots on the seat and asked, "What is that?" I told him, "My friend had a glass of water, and he threw it at the guys." The officer looked at me and said, "You are lucky they did not shoot you." I do not panic and remain calm under threat or pressure—a trait that has always served me well.

Later, talking to D. about the incident, he told me he had been in counterintelligence during the Korean War. "I have been in a lot of scary situations," he said, "but that one was probably the scariest. That is as close as I've come to truly fearing for my life."

Not long after that dinner, my husband and I looked at each other and said, "We have to move." We decided to look for a real house and wound up buying a place in Cheviot Hills. It was twenty-five hundred square feet. It felt like our palace.

***

Maybe because of his background, my husband did not seem threatened by my level of success. The life of a high-level, global corporate executive was not that different from the life he expected to live. Except he wasn't the high-level executive. I was.

For a long time, my husband worked for the same environmental company he'd joined when he first followed me to Southern California. He bounced around among several different positions in a handful of different locations—he worked out of the Bay Area for a while and even took a position in Florida at one point. Wherever he went, we made it work. I could tell at least one of the women who worked for him in Florida was coming on to him—there was actually no doubt in my mind. But I honestly did not think he did anything about it. I trusted him completely.

Still, he was chronically unhappy and unsatisfied with his job. Despite spending several years with the same company, despite his three degrees and his background and his obvious intelligence, he was never able to rise above the middle-management, not-particularly-well-compensated level. There was always a reason things didn't go his way. His bosses did not appreciate him. He was better and more competent than his bosses. Nobody understood him. The operation was badly run. It was a constant theme.

We had been talking about my husband leaving his job, but there was no way I was going to shoulder the expense of maintaining *Adventurous II* on my own while he looked for work. Then he sold the boat. So the next time he complained about his job, I told him, "Sweetheart, if you're this miserable at work, it's okay if you quit. You'll find something else." And just like that, he quit.

He wanted to do something entrepreneurial and began looking for opportunities. He found one on a Caltech trip we took with a group of professors, scientists, and other interesting, smart, accomplished people. With me facilitating some of the conversation, he met a Caltech professor who was aware of brilliant individuals who were developing new technologies and looking for investors to help commercialize and bring them to the market. There was another man who was wealthy with family money and interested in investing in new technologies. With their combined experiences, expertise, and connections, the three men started a small venture capital fund to invest in start-ups. My husband and I invested some of our money (meaning the money I worked hard to earn).

In theory, they had all the right components for success—technical know-how, connections, money, and my husband, who (supposedly) knew how to run a business. Unfortunately, while they worked with a few companies that were reasonably successful, at best the fund broke even. I will not for a moment suggest this was my husband's fault. I think they did everything that could be done to make it a success. But it was not. And that meant he never made any money.

At some point I told him, "It is fine that you're doing this, but your partners have other sources of income. So if you are going to devote yourself to this full time, then you need to get paid. And if you are not going to get paid for it, then you need to do what they are doing and go out and get another job, because this just is not right."

But my husband did not want to get another job. I was becoming more and more successful. I was a partner at a Big Four accounting and professional services firm, making more than enough money to support us both. Our lifestyle was not extravagant. Why did he need to get a job? Being in this so-called partnership and taking meetings, including the "standing meeting" he claimed to have at the Jet Propulsion Laboratory (JPL) every Monday night, played to his ego in a way another position as a middle manager, answering to a boss who no doubt would not appreciate him, would not.

In the end, he had twenty years working, which was a respectable career, but that was it. And he traded on those twenty years forever. It drove me crazy. We would be at an event, and he would tell people, "Oh, I'm an investor," or "I'm an entrepreneur," or "I'm a venture capitalist." It got to the point where I would secretly think, *You are nothing. You are at home doing nothing, and I am supporting you, and you are out here holding yourself out like this master of the universe.* He had charm, the pedigree, and the smarts, and he knew how to use them. He had good business skills. But something had gone off the rails for him. He was a complete phony.

In private, with me, he blamed it all on bad luck. He once said something along the lines of "If I'd just had a break or two, I would be running a major division of a company like General Electric." I thought, *And if I had been born into your family, where I had accomplished and well-connected people coaching, mentoring, and looking out for me—sending me to the right schools, giving me every opportunity, getting me in the best country clubs—I might have been president.*

I didn't say it out loud. But I thought it.

***

We had started sleeping in separate bedrooms. Part of it was that I was middle aged and going through perimenopause and was really, really struggling to sleep through the night. The other was that my husband was a horrible snorer, which made that challenge a million times more difficult. I would poke him so he would turn over and quiet down, and he would get mad at me. "Mary Ann, I need my rest, and you keep waking me up to ask me to roll over!" His total disregard for my feelings and my needs were a complete turnoff.

We were visiting Napa Valley with longtime friends of his, having dinner at the French Laundry, which is notoriously hard to get into. We had traveled to Napa with this couple several times before and tried to secure a reservation, never successfully. This trip, we were staying somewhere very, very close, and the concierge made a reservation. So, for the first and only time, I went to the French Laundry for dinner. The food was spectacular. The drinks were spectacular. Unfortunately, the conversation was very much not spectacular. Somehow, we got on the subject of religion, and one of our friends said something that made me very, very uncomfortable. Specifically, these two well-educated individuals (one was a highly regarded and successful neurologist and the other a classically trained and accomplished pianist) explained that you had to be a Christian to get into heaven.

I could not believe what I had heard, so I asked a few more questions, including, "Why is that?" My final question to them was this: "I want to be sure I understand. Are you telling me that if there is a Jewish person who has lived an exemplary life and a Christian who has led a life doing bad things, the Christian is going to heaven and the Jew is going to hell?" Their answer: "Yes." I remember almost nothing of our conversations, or the trip, after that moment. But I knew I would never see this couple again. My one and only meal at the French Laundry was ruined.

That night, my husband and I had sex, but for whatever reason, he was not satisfied. I honestly don't remember why. The next morning, I woke up to him shaking me. I looked at him to see what was wrong. He said, "Mary Ann, I want you."

I wasn't even awake yet. I said, "I am exhausted."

"I don't care," he said. "Do you not understand I need this now?"

It was a defining moment for me. Something about the way he expressed his desire ... there was almost a devilish feel to it. It was so self-absorbed and self-centered it bordered on *evil*. I do not remember what happened. I do not remember if we had sex. I do not remember if we didn't have sex. But I will never forget that at that moment, something changed for me. Our sex life was never the same after that. In fact, that may be the day it died.

***

A few years after that, my husband received a phone call. His mother got lost driving and had ended up on a freeway and off the side of the road—she apparently had blacked out and may have had a ministroke, but luckily she wasn't seriously hurt and did not hurt anybody else. Then they took her in for tests and found out she was consumed with cancer. This was the start of several months of my husband frequently going back and forth to Houston to see his mother. To take care of her.

I noticed his behavior was different. But I rationalized it. His mother was dying; he was going back and forth to care for her and that also meant dealing with dysfunction between him and his brother. I was traveling. Even though I knew things were not good, I thought the problem was mostly me. Perimenopause was not just affecting my sleep; it was affecting my emotions. It was like being a teenager again, except you cannot be a teenager at work, so I was trying to hold it together there and maybe losing control more and more at home. It affected my sex drive, too. Nothing was working like it used to work. Going through my mind were all these thoughts. *Okay, so things aren't great with us now, but you know what? I'm tired. I'm mad at him because he's not working. I don't know what's going on with me.* There was always part of me that thought, *At some level, I still love my husband, and I think it may still be okay. I think this may be one of those things that when I get through this, when he gets a job and starts contributing again, when I'm slightly more settled, when we're more comfortable, it will all be better.*

I could still see us as one of those couples walking on the beach holding hands in old age. How I thought that was all going to come back, I really had no idea.

At one point, he suggested we see a counselor, and I refused. I blamed it on being too busy, but I know one reason I did not want to go is that I did not want to know what I would find out. I never said that to him, and I would never fully admit it to myself, but I knew I was not ready to deal with what was happening in my marriage, because I knew I was not ready for another divorce. The one scenario I hung on to in my mind was *When I've got time, we'll sort through all this.*

***

My mother-in-law died in November 2002, which meant my husband and his brother had to split her estate and decide who got what. My husband was very practical about the whole thing. He did not want to bring home a random collection of furniture and tableware and accessories, so he videoed her entire house and made a list of exactly what was there. Then we hired a new interior designer, Hugo, to help us decide what would work in our house. I think Hugo and I have been working on something together ever since. He became and still is like a brother to me—chosen family.

Hugo went over the list with his expert eye, saying, "Get that; don't get that," and when we brought everything in, it looked sensational. A few years later we decided we should renovate and refresh the rest of the house. We ended up spending a ton of money to restucco the outside, remodel the kitchen, recarpet, purchase new furniture and reupholster certain pieces, Venetian plaster some rooms, and repaint others.

My husband had taken over paying all our bills, which was fine with me because I was so busy at work. My earnings were paid into the equivalent of a savings account, with interest, and I would transfer money to our joint checking account as needed to cover our expenses. I began to notice my husband asking for more and more money. "Mary Ann, I need you to transfer $25,000." "Mary Ann, I need you to transfer another $20,000." Finally, I asked him, "Where's all this money going?"

His answer was "We're redoing the house." That was true. It made sense.

But there were other signs that something was off. Once I woke up in the middle of the night and heard him going down the stairs. I got up and asked, "What's going on?" He was dressed to go out. He looked at me and said, "I'm going to the Magic Castle," which is a private club in LA he had recently joined. It was around ten o'clock at night, so it was early enough that it was plausible. But what married man gets up and gets dressed to go to a club in the middle of the night?

Another time, he was going down the stairs and turned to me and said, "I'm getting through this construction and that's it." That could have been taken a few different ways, but it hit me as a very odd comment at the time.

He decided to go see his brother over Labor Day to "work through some family matters," and he did not ask me to go. If he had asked me to go, I would have said no—I had reached my breaking point with his family years before, although I did go to his mother's funeral. But he was leaving again, and he had been doing less and less in the yard, which was the one thing he was still taking care of in addition to paying the bills. I was upset. So I complained.

I had been complaining more often by that point. Specifically, I had become more and more insistent about him finding a job. We fought about it constantly. "I'm not standing for this. You have got to go out and work. You've got to do more. This cannot just be all on me." At some point he did get a part-time consulting job that paid fairly well, and I assumed he was using that money to help with the bills. But since he handled all the money and I paid little or no attention, I did not really know where it was going.

***

It was a Monday night—December 1, 2008. One of my partners from the UK was flying in that day to join me for a client visit in Thousand Oaks on Tuesday. Thousand Oaks is a long drive from where we lived. My husband called me around five o'clock that evening, and I told him I would be picking up my partner at the airport and taking him to an early dinner, then picking him up early the next morning for the meeting in Thousand Oaks. It was a normal conversation (we still occasionally had those), and he was very nice on the phone. He reminded me he had his weekly standing Monday evening meeting at JPL. I said, "Okay. Well, if I don't see you tonight, I'll see you in the morning."

I arrived home from my early dinner and walked up the stairs to my bedroom. There were some papers sitting on the floor in the hallway in front of the bedroom door. On top of the papers, there was a Post-it note—a little yellow Carrie-Bradshaw-Berger-broke-up-with-me Post-it note.

I bent down and picked up the papers. The Post-it note read, "This isn't working. Please just sign. You can call me on my cell."

They were divorce papers. They had been filed in court that day. He never even told me he was talking to an attorney.

He never came home that night.

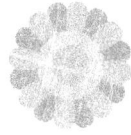

CHAPTER 6

DIVORCE COURT

I was blindsided. Completely stunned. I called five friends, all of whom I knew through the firm, and heard the same message from all of them. "Are you okay? Is there anything I can do for you? I will be here for you through this and when it's over. Did you see this coming?" Because that's just natural. "Did you have any idea?"

And finally, "Do not do anything before you talk to an attorney."

I called my friend Jim, who as I write is a distinguished, successful, and long-serving partner at the firm. He had worked for me almost from the day he started after graduating from university. He was in the middle of his own divorce. I said, "I need you to come over."

"MAC," he said, "I'm tired. It's been a long, hard day. I'm on my way home." He lived in Redondo Beach—about forty-five minutes from me.

"Please," I said. "I need you to come over."

He said, "Okay, I'll turn around. I'll be right there."

Jim came over, and I showed him the papers and the Post-it note. "What do I do?"

"Mary Ann," he said, "you need to find yourself a good attorney. And when you talk to them, here's all the things you need to let them know." He indicated the papers. "You need to let them know who his attorney is. Everything that's here. And don't you dare sign anything."

I did not.

I called my friend B., who was the managing partner for my region at that time. I told him what had happened and about my meeting in Thousand Oaks the next morning. He told me to cancel it. I told him I could not and that I would pull it together.

Again, he said, "You can cancel."

"Nope," I said. "I'll get through it. If I don't think I can pull this off, I will let you know, and we'll find somebody to cover."

I knew that was not going to happen. I was not going to let it happen.

A couple of times on Tuesday, my partner from the UK looked at me and asked, "Are you okay?"

"Oh, I'm fine," I said. "I'm just a little tired today." I know he had no idea.

***

At two or three in the morning on Tuesday it hit me. *Mary Ann, you're a very important partner at a Big Four firm. You are friends with the head of Partner Affairs, and you have a very good working relationship with the head of the firm's Office of General Counsel! Your firm works with attorneys all over the country! They can tell you who you need to go to!*

I called the partner who ran Partner Affairs, and he said, "Mary Ann, I'm all over it." Later that morning, he put me in touch with Stacy, who became my divorce attorney. Stacy introduced me to her partner, Marc. She also put me in touch with a therapist named Lu, who became one of my dearest friends, to help me deal with the emotional fallout. Lu helped me develop the strategy and find the strength to manage through the divorce, to stay focused on treating it like a business transaction. Team Mary Ann was in place.

I continued the work of apprising everyone who should know of what had happened. This was especially difficult with our mutual friends. I remember agonizing over how to tell one particular friend I felt especially close to. I finally sent an email that announced we were getting a divorce, and I went on to say, "You were somebody who was friends with both of us, and I would never ask you to not be his friend. But you need to understand that you will not be able to be friends with both of us, because with what I have seen and what I am going through now, that's not possible for me."

I got a note back that said, "I have loved you and him both. I honestly hope that I can be Switzerland and be friends to both of you." It was obvious he had gotten to our mutual friend first. I wrote back that while I respected the decision, it would not be possible for me.

At that point, something must have clicked. They wrote back, "Mary Ann, I should have read between the lines. I am here for you, period. Full stop. Anything you need, I am here for you."

My friend Kelley had fewer illusions about my husband. Her focus was on whether I had gone back to check our credit card records. I said, "Kelley, what are you talking about?" I had never thought to pay any attention to them.

She said, "Mary Ann, something's going on, right?"

So I started looking through credit card statements. And very quickly I noticed a pattern. There would be a charge for a room at the Century Plaza Hotel, which was probably less than two miles from where my husband and I lived. The next day there would be a charge for flowers. And there would be a charge to the same jeweler where we always bought my jewelry. One month it would be hotel charge, flower charge, jewelry charge; another month it might be jewelry charge, hotel charge, flower charge. They always came in groups. There were also a lot of trips in addition to a lot of gifts. I remembered seeing things hidden in the garage that I always assumed were for me. I now began to realize, or at least suspect, that he was hiding things for his mistress.

I also realized what those standing Monday night meetings at JPL were probably all about. It was crushing. The entire time I had known my husband, I had been completely faithful—even after the sex stopped.

Stacy assumed a mistress was not the only thing my husband was hiding. "That man has another bank account somewhere," she said. I asked her how she knew. "He went to a top law firm," she explained. "These attorneys are not working for him without a retainer. You need to ask him where he got the money for the retainer."

Probably from that part-time consulting job, and perhaps some of those money transfers he'd kept requesting. He had no doubt been squirreling money away for months, just waiting until he had enough saved up to file for divorce.

Later, I met with Stacy, Marc, and the forensic accountant they'd brought in to help track down where my husband was hiding money. "This will be ugly," Stacy warned. "He's got top counsel in this city. This man is going for it. He is going to try to take you for everything he can."

But Marc said, "This is actually a very boring divorce because, one, there is not much money to be fighting over, and two, the law is cut and dried."

That was fine with me. Boring was good. I just wanted it done.

***

All this was going on while I was hitting the peak of my career. I remember being at a meeting or event with one of my partners, a man so plugged in he often told his story of meeting Vladimir Putin (before he was openly poisoning people and invading countries). He looked at me and said, "We are on the Global Board. We are rock stars!" I did not feel like a rock star. I was a PwC partner with demanding responsibilities in the midst of a very expensive divorce. I was really just trying to hold it all together.

My estranged husband, on the other hand, had no job. His full-time job was divorcing me. My full-time job paid for my attorneys, supported my husband, and, as I had discovered, supported his mistress, too.

At one point not long after he surprised me with divorce papers, my now-estranged husband approached me with an offer. "To save money, maybe I can stay at the house when you're not there. And other times I can bunk with a friend." What sixty-something-year-old-man bunks with a friend?

Once I realized that he had a mistress, I knew what he must have meant. I said, "I cannot live with you in this house. Take whatever you need and get out."

When I told Stacy what I had learned, she said, "I can't promise you, but we can try to get some of the money back in the settlement." But I needed help sorting through all the documents that would show where he'd spent money and what he'd spent it on, and I was already up to my eyeballs in things to do. So I called a friend, a very technical, detail-oriented person who knew how to use spreadsheets, and asked for her help. I told her I would buy her ticket and she could stay with me while she went through my husband's and my records and figured out how much of "our" money he had spent on other women. She got on a plane and came.

My friend teamed up with my former partner and friend, who retired before I did and still handles my taxes. Everything started falling into place. I remembered a family wedding we attended on the East Coast, not that long before we split. My husband and I were on the dance floor, and I noticed he was suddenly dancing like Fred Astaire. I was so taken off guard that I actually said, "Wow! When did you learn to dance like that?" Many times over the years I'd said I would love it if we took dance lessons. He would never agree to do so. When my friend went through our records, she discovered he had been taking dance lessons with his mistress. Which I had paid for.

He had taken her on a $15,000 trip to Belize, where we had spent our honeymoon, which I also paid for. I could list more surprises, but you get the idea. Altogether, my friend and my former partner were able to uncover almost $400,000 that my husband had spent on his mistress (or mistresses—who knows?). While I had been working to support us, he was out lavishly spending that money on other women.

Thank goodness I had that company account in which all my earnings were directly deposited. This meant my husband always had to ask me to transfer money to our joint account. There is no doubt in my mind it would have been worse had this not been the case. Because he had to ask. He had to have some plausible explanation, like redoing the house, in order for me to give him that much money. He had inherited a small amount from his mother that at some point he'd combined with our joint account. In retrospect, I think he did that to obfuscate.

I felt so stupid. But my forensic accountant said, "The one thing I will not let you do is blame yourself for trusting the person you were married to. Don't go there. Don't beat yourself up. You were married to this man. Even with what you know now, you don't get to beat yourself up for having trusted the person you were married to."

In the meantime, I had Lu, my therapist, coaching as well as counseling me. Lu was therapist to the stars and many other high-profile individuals and had seen countless complicated, ugly, really expensive divorces over the decades. Still, when I told her my story, she said, "Mary Ann, I have never seen anything like this. No one with a conscience could do what this man has done." So at that point, I started reading everything I could about people without a conscience, starting with a book by Robert D. Hare.

One of the many smart things Lu did was recommend that my husband and I see another therapist together. He agreed to do so, and he had his own therapist, too. We only saw Dr. J. for a month, but I am very glad we did. I benefited immensely from the experience. I remember at the first session, he said it was hard to overcome the damage done by infidelity. He told us the odds were against us staying together. The sessions with Dr. J. helped me realize, and at times I still remind myself, that there is nothing I could have done to save the marriage.

I knew my husband was going to try to manipulate Dr. J., just as he had manipulated our first therapist twenty-plus years before. I was not wrong. Early on, Dr. J. said, "You both told me you are seeing your individual therapists. Let me know if it's okay for me to talk to them." I immediately said, "Absolutely. You may share anything with Lu. Please do." But my husband said, "That's a really good question. I need to think about that."

By that point I had read enough about individuals without a conscience that I grasped the fact that anything is possible. My husband could lie with the most amazing ease. And he had guns. He had lots of guns. Including an AK-47-type gun that was illegal in California.

In one session, he told Dr. J. about a fight we'd had during which I'd ripped the pocket of his shirt and that this had made him afraid of me being violent and hurting him. Dr. J. said, "I take any hint of violence very seriously." I admitted that indeed I had ripped his shirt, and thought to myself it was crazy that either of them would think or suggest I could or would physically hurt him. I told Lu about this at our next session, and she laughed and said he deserved much worse than me tearing his shirt. Lu had the most wonderful laugh ...

Toward the end of one session, I finally said to my estranged husband, "You have guns. Would you hurt me?"

"Mary Ann, I love you," he said. "I love you."

"Yes," I said, "but would you hurt me?" He did not say anything.

The session ended, and Dr. J. said, "This is where we will pick up next time."

A week later, Dr. J. said, "We're going back to where we left off. Mary Ann, you asked your husband a question. Do you want to repeat it?"

I asked him again if he would use his guns to hurt me.

My husband said, "I don't know why you would ask that. I know all about guns. I've had guns my whole life. I'm trained in gun safety. I know how to use a gun."

Dr. J. said, "That's not what she asked you."

My husband would not say he would not hurt me. Dr. J. tried two or three more times. He kept coming back to it. But he would never respond to the question.

One of the things Hare noted in his book was that people without a conscience often use contradictory and inconsistent statements that usually escape detection. He gave several examples, including this one: When asked if he had ever committed a crime, a violent offense, a man serving time for theft answered, "No, but I once had to kill someone." And this one: A man serving a term for armed robbery replied to the testimony of an eyewitness, "He's lying. I wasn't there. I should have blown his fucking head off."

There was that disconnect. My husband said, "I know all about guns. I know how to use guns. I know about gun safety. I love you." But he would not say, "I would not hurt you." It was disquieting and scary.

Since Dr. J. had my permission to talk to Lu, she was able to fill me in on what he told her. She told me Dr. J. believed that my estranged husband was a person without a conscience and that, based on what I had told her and on Dr. J.'s observations, she agreed with that assessment. Lu explained to me that such people are such extraordinary liars that they regularly fool psychological professionals. Because Dr. J. spent time with us together, he was better able to "see under the mask."

At one point, my husband tried to get Dr. J. to see him separately. "You know, Dr. J.," he said, "next week my therapist is going to be out of town. Could I maybe see you? Because right now, this is just really a tough time." Dr. J. turned him down. It didn't end up mattering, because before the month was over, we were done with Dr. J. I told my husband I was finished, that Dr. J. would not be able to get us past this, and that we needed to proceed with the divorce.

Still, I am glad I we saw Dr. J. as a couple. Thanks to those sessions, it became clear to me who my husband was. At one point during one of our sessions, I realized I did not know him at all. *I have been living with this person for over twenty years, and I don't know who he is.* So I took my forensic accountant's advice and did not second-guess myself about how I could have loved a person like my second husband. I trusted the man I married, and I know there is no shame in that.

***

My estranged husband kept obstructing the divorce process, which made ending our marriage more and more expensive. We had to take him to court to get him to sign the listing on the house, which we needed to sell. Stacy told me the judge was not pleased and said something to my husband and his counsel along the lines of "I'm watching you." It was during the Great Recession of 2009, but we almost immediately received an offer that was equal to the listing price. Unfortunately the buyers backed out within two weeks. We immediately listed again and soon received another offer at the same listing price. Our Realtor was a star.

The buyers' inspector found that something needed to be done to the roof. They asked for $6,000 off the price to cover it—something that, if you have ever sold a house, is completely normal and comes with the territory. My husband said, "No. And if they walk away, fine."

The list and accepted offer price of the house was $1,500,000, and he was willing to risk the sale over $6,000. In September 2009.

He blamed me for putting us in this situation. He accused me of letting the house fall into disrepair. When it was clear I was not buying what he was selling, he moved to "If this falls through, I'm sure somebody else will come along and pay even more for it." I thought, *You have got to be kidding.* We were in the middle of the biggest economic crisis of our lifetimes. We were lucky to sell, and to sell so quickly.

That Realtor was smart. He offered to split the $6,000 with us fifty-fifty—he would pay $3,000, and my estranged husband and I would each pay $1,500. He paid more than we did individually. It was just so stupid. But it worked. The house sale closed in either November or December, almost a year after I'd come home to divorce papers and a Post-it note. That November, I bought an apartment near

Century City. A good friend flew in from Paris, and she and Hugo helped me move. It is still my home today.

Even then, my hopefully soon-to-be ex-husband was not done making trouble. Instead of splitting the proceeds from the house immediately so we would both have the money, he insisted that we put it in escrow until the divorce was final. Almost every dollar I had was going to pay my attorneys, spousal support to my estranged husband, and all my other living expenses. I would wake up in the morning and immediately start thinking, *I am near bankruptcy and going to have no money when I come out of this. I cannot declare bankruptcy. I am a PwC partner. I am on the global board.*

There had been a point earlier in the process where we reached a voluntary settlement agreement, or VSA. We worked with a mediator, a retired judge whom I will call RJ. He came to Stacy's office and started by meeting with Stacy and me and then met with my estranged husband and his attorney, who were sequestered in another room. Stacy also went back and forth. RJ's approach was to work only with the attorneys and individually with the spouses; he would not let my estranged husband and me see one another. In retrospect, I can see how much sense that made, trying to help us reach a settlement while keeping us separated, so we could not push each other's buttons or otherwise obstruct the process.

RJ started by drawing something on a piece of paper and then handing it to me. "Here's a pie," he said, showing me the drawing. "This pie is your assets. The pie will not get bigger."

Then he said, "Until you settle, all that will happen is that you will keep spending money on attorneys. The attorneys will get their piece of the pie first. Your piece and your husband's piece will get smaller and smaller." I am sure he had the same discussion with my husband.

At one point later in the day, RJ and I were talking about the alimony I would have to pay my husband. By this point he had spent hours with both of us, and we were on a first-name basis. "J.," I said, "this man has three degrees. From what I understand about alimony, you take into account what he should be able to earn by getting a job? He can't just *not* go look for a job, can he? Look at him on paper, and look at me!"

RJ looked at me. "Mary Ann," he said, "let me explain it to you this way. Let's assume for a moment this is a horse race. Let me assure you, nobody is betting on him. You are the horse that everyone is betting on."

Suddenly, I understood. Plus there was the fact that my husband was sixty-five years old. "I got it," I said. "Thank you very much for that, J." We reached an agreement that day. Or that night. It was eight or nine in the evening by the time we were done.

My soon-to-be ex-husband's lawyer said, "We can write it up tomorrow," but Stacy and I insisted on writing it up before we left. His attorney wrote the agreement by hand, and we both signed. Everything would be typed up in the next day or so. That was all we needed—the formal, final typed agreement and the signatures. Then we could both move on with our lives.

Except when we received the final, formal document, my about-to-be ex-husband would not sign. And he would not sign, and he would not sign, and he would not sign.

Weeks went by. At some point he admitted, "I'm not going to live by this. I don't agree with it." It turned out he had signer's remorse over the settlement we had reached regarding my retirement plan. As I recall, that portion of the overall settlement was proposed by his attorney with his agreement. That was when he moved on to attorney number two.

It kept getting worse. He changed attorneys a total of four times, and every time he did, we had to re-cover old ground, and of course this cost more money. Every time we dealt with something in court, it cost me tens of thousands of dollars. Stacy had warned me from the beginning, "Just remember, you're both going to have less after this is over." I was watching my bank balance get smaller and smaller every single month. I was going to end up with nothing.

One day Marc called and said, "Mary Ann, I've got good news and bad news." Before I could say I wanted the bad news first, he said, "The good news is, I know a really good appellate attorney."

Appellate attorney? That meant the bad news must be really bad. I asked Marc what the bad news was.

"Well, Mary Ann," he said, "we have a 'matter of first impression.'" I knew what this meant—there was no legal precedent on point. He went on, "We think the written agreement you've got is enforceable, but it is not clear cut. I want you to talk to an appellate attorney." Which, of course, would cost me another few thousand dollars.

I met with the appellate attorney. "Nothing's ever black and white," he said, "but I think you've got a really good case if we need to go to appeal."

I called Marc. "Do you remember when I first met you and you told me this was a boring case?" I asked. "Because there wasn't enough money and the legal issues were not interesting?"

"I do, Mary Ann."

"So," I asked him, "what do you think right now?"

"Mary Ann, your case is an attorney's wet dream. It's fascinating."

Stacy agreed. At one point, she said, "I wish you had more money, because this would be fascinating to take to appeal. I think we would win and the original agreement would be enforced." I wished I had more money, too, and I am sure my husband would have found a way to spend it and take it. His divorce filing sounded like he was the spurned wife of a rich Hollywood mogul. "She is a partner, we traveled in style, there were cars to meet us everywhere." We went to some meetings, but it wasn't *Lifestyles of the Rich and Famous*. It was my job.

I read *Eat, Pray, Love*, which had been published a few years earlier. Did I finish it? I don't know. I do know I wanted to throw it across the room because it made me so angry. If you somehow managed to avoid it, it's the story of a writer who gets divorced and goes on a "journey of discovery" to Italy (where she eats), India (where she prays), and Indonesia (where she falls in love). I remember thinking, *Seriously? I am worried about bankruptcy and managing my career, and you're hanging out eating good food and meditating?* Anybody who reads that book thinking it is anything close to what it is like to go through a divorce does not live in the world I lived in.

My life was more like *Work, Try to Sleep, Get through This Divorce.* I would get up in the morning and go to work, come home, go to sleep, and do it all over again the next day. I'd have a meltdown every now and then, but not often. One I remember happened when I was at a board meeting in New York. In the middle of the meeting, I got a text or an email from my attorney saying, "Please call me ASAP." I thought, *Oh no, he's done something else.* I don't remember what specific horrible thing he had done that time. But I know it was bad enough that I had to get up and leave the room.

I walked into the office of my friend who was the head of Partner Affairs. It was around the corner from the boardroom on the twenty-fourth floor. I shut door and said, "Would you excuse me? I just need to break down for a moment ..." And I sat there and cried for a minute or two. Then I said, "I'm okay now." I cleaned my face, and I got up and went back into the boardroom.

In retrospect, I think my husband made everything difficult because he did not really want to stop being my husband. I think he wanted me to throw in the towel and behave. I do not know this for certain, but I think he hoped I would just give up and go back to having sex with him, get off his case about getting a job, and settle back into some version of our former life. He had already proved to himself that he could fool me, and who knows how long he had been doing that? He probably assumed he could get whatever he needed on the side, so it would be a win-win for him. Or maybe at some point he just realized, *My lifestyle is not going to be as good without her as it is with her.*

***

The longer the case dragged on, the more my estranged husband antagonized everyone. It appeared his attorneys did not like him. He stiffed his first lawyers. At one point, he had to pay my attorney's fees for one of the hearings. Stacy told me that rarely happened, that whatever gives rise to this sanction generally goes on a "list" and is addressed as part of the final settlement. On day one she and Marc had warned me that I might have to pay my husband's attorney's fees because he was a sixty-five-year-old man without a job or other income and that divorce in California is 100 percent no fault. The fact that he had to pay some of my fees, even once, suggests he did something egregious. Later, at another hearing, the judge put him on notice that if he did not behave, he was in danger of paying *all* my legal fees.

I was with Stacy when she deposed his forensic accountant. As I watched and listened, with my estranged husband's attorney looking distracted and uninterested on the other side of the table, I had a sense they both liked me more than their own client. I heard an audible gasp from his forensic accountant when she saw the total of my legal fees to date.

I think that forensic accountant was one of the few people my estranged husband respected. That was the other thing I learned about people without a conscience: they trust very few people. But this accountant was someone he trusted. I will never know, but I wondered if she went back and said, "What are you doing? If you end up having to pay her legal fees, you will have nothing."

Early one morning, not long after that, I arrived at my office to a voicemail message from my estranged husband. "Mary Ann, this is crazy," he said. "We are to the point where the attorneys are going to get everything." And he asked how I would feel if we asked a mutual friend we both trusted to help us sort through everything.

We contacted this friend, who was smart, kind, and levelheaded. She had been our neighbor when we lived in that small townhouse on Olympic Boulevard, had moved to Houston for work before we moved to Cheviot Hills, and was at that point retired and living in Paris.

I called Marc and told him. He said, "Go for it."

I sent our friend an email, and she agreed to come and serve as our mediator. I told my soon-to-be ex that I would use my airline miles for her flight. He offered to reimburse me for half the value of the ticket and did. She stayed with me at my apartment. We met in a conference room with a harbor view at the Marina Del Rey hotel where my estranged husband was staying. The first thing our friend did was disclose that she had helped me move. We both wanted to be transparent about this and ensure it did not shake his trust in her, which it did not.

The three of us sat there and hammered out an agreement. One of the first things my soon-to-be ex asked about was alimony. According to the DissoMaster, the standard by which such things are calculated in

California, he was entitled to about $17,000 a month. It was very black and white. He said, "Mary Ann, I will do this. I will settle for $10,000 a month. But I want it to go on even if I get married." I agreed.

When I later told Stacy, she objected. "But, Mary Ann, if he marries, or even if he's living with somebody, you don't have to pay!" This was true. But I was treating this as a business transaction. I was going to retire in five years—that was company policy. That meant, whether he remarried or not, the alimony payments would end. I said, "Stacy, this man is smart. He is not going to get married. And for me to prove he is living with somebody, I will have to hire a private investigator, we will end up back in court, you will have to do depositions. It is cheaper for me to pay him the $10,000 a month for five years. It is tax deductible. So, yes, I know I don't have to do it, but I am going to do it."

My soon-to-be ex obsessed over the idea of me keeping any "family" items. I had some of his mother's jewelry, which was gorgeous, including a stunning and very valuable piece she'd inherited from an aunt. She left it to me in her will, which made it my separate property. There was also a beautiful C. M. Russell sculpture that my husband's uncle had given us. The sculpture was very meaningful to me because of whom it came from. I told my estranged husband, "I promise I will leave that to whomever you want. You tell me. Wherever you want the family jewelry to go, I will do that in my will."

I also said, "I am prepared to back off on the Russell sculpture if that will facilitate us getting this done. You know what your uncle meant to me, and I would love to have it for that reason, but you can have the sculpture if it helps us get this finalized."

He said, "Keep it." One of a series of surprisingly decent things he did that day.

With agreement on the alimony and personal property, the big remaining issue was my retirement plans. Under California law, my ex would be entitled to a portion of my retirement. There was nothing I could do about that. Pensions are considered property, and the way his share was determined was formulaic. The formula said I would have to pay him 36.71 percent of my retirement payment every month for the rest of my life. If I got hit by a truck, he would be SOL, because PwC pays only to the retired partner, and the payments stop when the retired partner dies. However, if he predeceased me, by law I would have been obligated to continue to pay almost 37 percent of my pension to his estate until the day I died. That rankled me.

I looked at him and said, "The one thing that is truly troubling to me is the fact that if you predecease me, I will have to continue to pay your estate. If we had children, I'd be okay with that. But we don't."

After a pause, I continued, "So ... will you agree that if you predecease me, the payments from my retirement plan will stop on that date?"

He quickly and graciously agreed. I was ecstatic and grateful. I do not remember when, but during the process he agreed to reduce what he received in the settlement by the amount we had shown he spent on his mistress. Everything he did that day, in that Marina Del Rey hotel conference room with a view of the harbor, was decent. Does it make up for everything else? No. But I believe we finalized the agreement in the best way possible for both of us.

Lu had advised me to have clearly written in the agreement that it was final in all respects and that neither party had the right to come back for anything in the future. That made it in there too.

One evening, a few days before we were scheduled for the "all hands" meeting to finalize the agreement, my almost ex-husband left a voice message, again on my office phone. "Mary Ann, you don't even have to respond to this message if you don't want to. But I am calling to see if there is any way this can end other than in divorce."

I listened to the message and thought, *We have got to get through this.* My business head was working overtime. I left him a voicemail. I said, "I received your message, and I really appreciate that. I think the best thing we can do, so that we can possibly have any relationship going forward, is for us to finish this as quickly and amicably as we can."

The process went on. There was the "all hands" phone call with me, Marc, my almost-ex-husband's attorneys from whatever top-tier family law firm he was with at the time, plus his business attorney, his forensic accountant, and my forensic accountant. It was early in the morning, and we were going through the final details.

We were not working with the typical, standard divorce form, because instead of having his family law counsel draft the agreement, my soon-to-be ex had it drafted by his business attorney. That was why he was on the call. We had all read the agreement, it looked good to me, and no one on the other side objected. The end was in sight. I just had to get us there.

I said, "We both need to agree this is it. Done. Final. Neither of us can come back on anything." I even promised him I would get my will done within six months. Marc said I didn't have to do that, but I didn't care. "Why not?" I asked. "I need to do it anyway. It's a deadline. It's good motivation." And thanks to our mutual friend who'd come in from Paris, and probably his forensic accountant, my husband agreed to the terms by which he would become my ex-husband. The last step was to get it signed by the judge and properly recorded in the records. We would finally be divorced.

At one point during the call, somebody was saying something and I said, "Stop. Wait a minute. I want to hear from his family law attorney. I want to make sure you're okay with this language." I heard his forensic accountant chuckling in the background. I suspect she recognized I was managing the meeting. It was a transaction that I very much wanted to happen, and I was doing whatever I had to do to see it through to the end.

When finalized by the court, the process had taken just over nineteen months. I'd come home to the Post-it note on December 1, 2008, and the divorce was final on July 16, 2010.

I did not have to pay his attorney's fees. I am grateful for that, because unlike my now ex-husband, I could never walk away from my obligations. Who knows how many hundreds of thousands of dollars this would have cost me? I never added it all up. I never wanted to know exactly how much I paid Stacy, Marc, and their firm. Way too much, that I know. But I am convinced that all the pain and drama and expense was just part of my journey, and it brought me to all these other wonderful things in my life.

That does not mean I was brimming with gratitude toward the man who'd come to be known by all my friends as Evil Bastard, or EB for short. For a long time I added a touch of snark to his alimony checks. Part of our agreement was that my alimony payment would be reduced by any income over a certain dollar amount, whatever the source of that income, including getting paid to work. Arguably he was required to try to find a job, but he was over sixty-five and I had no realistic way to enforce this. Still, I had this silly hope that he might decide he wanted to work again, for whatever reason. What can I say—I am a hopeful person? I thought maybe, with me finally out of the picture, he might want to recapture some shred of dignity. To this day, virtually any male to whom I tell the story, whether friend or business colleague, says, "What kind of man would do this? No real man would do nothing and let himself be supported." Regardless, he had to account to me quarterly until the alimony stopped when I retired. So I would send snarky notes like "Got a job yet?" or "How's that job hunt going?" along with the checks. Not that I trusted he would give me legitimate information if he did get a job.

The only time I really went ballistic was when I learned, sometime before the alimony stopped, that Evil Bastard had leased a Porsche. I guess that was where he got his dignity. I knew leasing a Porsche had to cost $3,000 or $4,000 a month. I also knew in general what his rent and his other expenses were, because he had to provide me with an accounting of all his income, including copies of his bank statements. That meant he still had some money stashed away or was having to use some of the money he'd received in the settlement. I, on the other hand, had spent everything I had on attorney's fees and to buy my new apartment. EB had half my 401(k) and half the proceeds from the sale of the house. I worked all my life for those things, and he took them.

But that, I think, is the irony of this whole story. Everything my ex-husband ended up with, everything he has now, everything he uses to feed his ego and prop himself up and impress people, he got from me. He came into the world privileged. Whatever the reason, he never managed to build the successful business career he tried to present and never did what he needed to do to support himself. Or maybe he did. He married a nobody from Mart, Texas, who supports him to this day.

One night during this nineteen-month process, as I was beginning to grasp who Evil Bastard was, I had a vivid dream. I saw him going down a spiral staircase to the gates of hell. He had the look of a devil on his face. I saw the evil.

Then again, I had already seen it. I just did not recognize it right away.

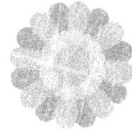

CHAPTER 7

NEW YORK

I had achieved more in my career than I even knew to aspire to when I first started … but I was not done. I once told one of the partners whom I reported to in New York that I would be willing to transfer anywhere, especially New York, and his response was something along the lines of "I don't know if you could deal with New Yorkers." I do not know what gave him that impression—whether it was because traces of my Texas accent still surface at times (I am told), because I had what I believe to be a quiet and gracious way of dealing with conflict, or because I was a petite woman who had never lived anywhere but Texas and California. While I did not know what gave this partner that impression of me, I thought I would handle New York well. While we were still married, I once asked EB how he would feel about a transfer to New York. He was quick to let me know that he had no interest whatsoever in moving.

Well, now I was divorced. Evil Bastard's opinion no longer mattered. I let our CEO and other members of his senior leadership team know that I was interested in the position as head of PwC's

Governance Insights Center. It was the first time in my career that I had specifically and emphatically let people know that I wanted a position. When they made me the offer, I was beyond thrilled. Since I was within five years of retirement, the company treated it as a temporary assignment instead of a relocation requiring me to sell my apartment in Los Angeles. This was the standard and most cost-effective approach for the firm, and perfect for me. I had the standard living allowance to help cover my expenses; was given the opportunity to do something professionally exciting, challenging, and different; and would have the experience of living on the East Coast. All without having to give up my home in LA.

I had no idea I would stay forever.

I spent the first two years in Morristown, New Jersey, near the office where everyone reporting to me was based. I could have lived in Manhattan and commuted, but I knew myself well enough to worry that if I lived in New York City, I would find reasons not to go to New Jersey, and I knew that I needed to be there regularly. Hugo found an apartment across the street from the Morristown Green and once again made it mine and moved me in. It was lovely, warm, and comfortable, but I was traveling much of the time. New Jersey never became a second home.

Then it was early 2014, and I had slightly more than a year before my mandatory retirement on June 30, 2015, having turned sixty the previous October. I realized this was my last chance to live in Manhattan while I was still an active PwC partner. It would be for only a year and was a manageable financial commitment. I called Hugo and asked him what he thought, and he said, "Let's do it." One morning I left my New Jersey apartment for a ten-day business trip and returned to my new apartment on the Upper West Side of New York City. Hugo had everything perfectly set up. I walked in, and I was home. I kept my apartment in LA, but New York quickly became my real home.

I now say I've always been a New Yorker; it just took me a long time to actually live in New York City ... although it did take a while for me to fully assimilate. Before I moved here, I was intimidated by the subway and never took it unless someone was with me. I had never been on a New York City bus. At the same time, hailing a cab in the middle of the crowded city terrified me. I am proud that today I can hail a cab like a native and regularly use public transportation.

Despite the distance, I stayed close to my friends in LA and around the world. It became clear during the divorce and in its aftermath that those friends were my fortress. They literally encircled me. No man was going to get inside those walls and hurt me again—at least not if they had anything to say about it. One friend gave the group a name—Friends of Mary Ann Cloyd, or FOMAC. Each of these loving, loyal, dependable, and protective friends know who they are, coast to coast and in between and across oceans. They were by my side, each in their own way, as I worked through the divorce and the rest of that chapter of my life. And they remained that way to make sure there never, ever was another Evil Bastard in my life.

***

My job running the Governance Insights Center required interacting with companies' boards and executives, the highest levels of corporate America and around the world. It was a high-profile position. I regularly participated in events, often speaking and presenting to successful and prominent individuals. One of them, Mr. X., was chairman of the board of a well-known company. At one event we discussed meeting for dinner and agreed that we would find a time to do so in the near future.

In some respects, my dinner with Mr. X. was similar to that first lunch with Evil Bastard, except for physical appearance and the part where EB walked off the elevator and I instantly thought this was a man I would marry. Mr. X. was no Cary Grant. He was a relatively attractive Black man, but no Sidney Poitier or Denzel Washington. However, he was smart, engaging, and interesting. And just like with EB, we connected immediately, albeit strictly on a professional, get-to-know-you level. We shared our backstories. I told him I was divorced, and he told me he had never been married, which surprised me. Most men I knew like Mr. X., highly successful executives in their late fifties or early sixties, had been married at least once. I was so surprised that I asked him how it was that he had never married. He blamed it on having always been hyper focused on his career and becoming a successful businessman. He said he had been so busy working it had never happened.

After that dinner, he invited me to speak in front of the board he chaired. I traveled to his office to meet. He filled me in on the challenges that existed with the board, how he thought I might be able to help, and what I might present.

We met a few times while preparing for the meeting, and I met the company's general counsel and corporate secretary. This was very typical. The executives and directors bringing you in to speak to a board are understandably protective about what you are going to cover and how you are going to cover it. I must have passed inspection, because I received the green light to come and present. I remember that it went well. I was good at what I did, and everyone was engaged. It was a successful meeting.

Mr. X. and I stayed in touch and became friends. Almost from the first time we met, there had been an intense intellectual and spiritual connection. We had a lot in common. Like me, he grew up without a lot of money. I do not know if he was raised by his grandparents, but his grandmother was a very influential and important part of his life. He told me she had worked as "a domestic," meaning she cleaned for people. I vaguely recall my grandmother having worked in a bakery before staying home full time to take care of me, and my grandfather was a mechanic who worked in a garage and would come home dirty with grease under his fingernails. I could relate to this man who'd come from nothing and, like me, was making his way in a world run mostly by privileged white men.

I was impressed by Mr. X.'s accomplishments. He was highly educated, with a law degree and MBA from an Ivy League school. He told me he'd worked for several years at a good law firm but then pivoted and launched his own company, where he began his rise through the ranks in the business world. He was prominent and connected, including politically. He had served in several appointed positions, both city and federal, including some requiring a presidential appointment and Senate confirmation. His pedigree was amazing.

Mr. X. and I did not see each other often, but because we moved in the same business circles and had connections with the same organizations, we would often be at the same events. At one such event—I was probably on a panel, or maybe he was, or maybe we both were—we passed each other walking in opposite directions. As we reached out to shake hands, there was a spark. Like electricity. A physical jolt. We were not on carpet. It was outside, and it was spring, summer, or fall, so there was no mistaking it. It took me by surprise. *Whoa. Wow, what was that?* We had plans to get together for dinner that night, but Mr. X. called me and canceled, saying he had too much on his plate. I knew he was busy, and so was I.

I started catching myself thinking about Mr. X. when we were not together. Once, standing at the kitchen counter in my New Jersey apartment, I sent him an email or a text—I don't remember how we communicated back then—that just said, "Thinking of you." Within a minute, he called me. He said, "I got your note. I pulled over to call you." That surprised me. When I brought it up with Lu, she said, "Mary Ann, 'thinking of you'? How many cards have you seen that say 'thinking of you'?"

But I wasn't thinking of Mr. X. *that* way! After EB, I had zero interest in sex, dating, or anything resembling intimacy of any kind with a man. I was too raw and wounded after what I had been through. And honestly, I never thought that was what my relationship with Mr. X. was about. We were just good friends. Yes, he did send me beautiful flowers at the office, and everyone noticed, especially my executive assistant, but I thought it was just a gesture of friendship.

Then one day, after I had moved to Manhattan, Mr. X. came to New York, I thought on business. We met for dinner at Café Luxembourg, one of my favorite Upper West Side neighborhood places that first opened its doors in 1983. We were enjoying our meal when he suddenly looked at me and said, "Mary Ann, don't you know I'm courting you?"

I was floored.

Until that moment, I do not think I had considered the prospect of dating anyone. My heart was shut. I had not had sex with anybody in a very, very long time—I had not been with another man since that day, approximately thirty years before, when I met EB in Dallas. The thought of having sex terrified me at that point. But I trusted Mr. X. I felt I could be honest with him, so I was. I explained that I did not know if I could have a physical relationship with him. I really did not. It was not like it had been with EB, where there was this immediate, intense physical attraction. But we had a deep friendship, and Mr. X.

was very, very patient. He did not demand sex from me. He did not demand anything …

And before I knew it, I was "seeing someone."

I was slow to share my secret. In the early days of "being courted," I told only some of my close friends and my executive assistant, who managed my life and of course knew about the flowers. She and I were close on a personal as well as professional basis. She was the consummate EA and friend, could be trusted in every way, kept confidences.

One day I had a business lunch with Mr. G., who was a well-known figure in the world of corporate governance. He knew Mr. X., and both Mr. X. and I had attended and presented at the organization's events. For some reason we were talking about Mr. X., and he mentioned something about Mr. X.'s "estranged wife." That made no sense. At that very first dinner, Mr. X. had told me he had never been married. I did not mention this to Mr. G. The minute I was back in the privacy of my office, I called Mr. X. and told him that Mr. G. had mentioned his "wife."

"What?" said Mr. X. "I don't have a wife!"

We tried to figure out where Mr. G. might have gotten this idea. Was he confusing Mr. X. with another Black corporate leader with a troubled marriage? Mr. X.'s voice registered annoyance, perhaps some anger, understandably, wondering out loud if Mr. G. got his Black men mixed up.

We were at another restaurant, I don't remember which one, the first time Mr. X. told me he loved me. He looked at me and said, "Don't say it back. I'm not asking you to." He was so understanding about my intimacy issues. Of course, we had many conversations about my ex-husband and his lack of a conscience. He even knew about his nickname, Evil Bastard. So after telling me he loved me, he said, "It doesn't matter. I love you enough. We don't even have to have sex." Which was good, because we still hadn't. But it was okay. I had never felt so totally accepted, even with my discomfort around sex.

I began to tell FOMAC about Mr. X., and to a person they gave their approval. Lu said, "Mary Ann, for the first time, you're dating a *real man* who is genuinely successful in business." Ms. L. was the first FOMAC member to meet him in person. She was in New York for work, and the three of us met for dinner. Ms. L. and Mr. X. had an immediate connection. She was an attorney, a litigator at a white-shoe law firm. At one time she had been a state prosecutor, before she went into private practice. During our conversation, Mr. X. asked her if she was the same Ms. L. who had successfully prosecuted a case in which she artfully handled getting a child to testify, on the witness stand, against a parent. She was, in fact, *that* Ms. L. Later I went to the bathroom, and when I came back, Mr. X. was gone and Ms. L. was alone at the table. She looked at me and said, "Mary Ann, this man loves you. Just go with it. Don't be stupid."

A few months later, we were in yet another New York restaurant when Mr. X. asked me to marry him. He actually wrote it on a piece of personalized notepaper he carried in his pocket. He didn't have a ring. I asked, "Are you serious?" We still hadn't had sex! I was already a two-time divorcée. We were having such a wonderful time—if we married, how would we keep it alive and fresh?

I texted Ms. L., "Mr. X. just proposed to me." She texted back, "Say yes, say yes, say yes." I looked at the text and thought, *I guess I say yes.* I told Lu and Kellee, Lu's daughter, who is also a licensed therapist and a dear friend, and everybody said the same thing: "This makes such complete sense." Even when I reminded Lu that we hadn't had sex yet, she said, "You'll get there." Lu knew me better than anyone, and I trusted her.

I said yes.

By this point in my life, Lu was so much more than my therapist. She was one of my very dearest friends. We had a special connection from the moment we met. After I moved to the East Coast, I did not see her often, but every time I was back in LA, if at all possible I would schedule time. She often worked from her home office.

One afternoon, I arrived at Lu's home for a session, walked up the steep front steps, and rang the doorbell. Her housekeeper opened the door, invited me in, and said I should join Lu in the kitchen. I walked in, and Lu was sitting on a kitchen stool with her phone in front of her. She said she needed a glass of wine—"There's some in the refrigerator—would you please pour me a glass?" She asked if I would like one, too. I declined. Then she looked at me and said, "I just got off the phone with the doctor. The cancer's back."

Lu had had breast cancer many, many years before I knew her. It was treated aggressively and successfully, but that led to other health issues as a direct result of the radiation she received. What were the odds I would be the person who showed up in her home just as she finished the call with her doctor? This wonderful woman to whom I was so connected—I do not believe it was a coincidence. I felt fortunate to be there in that moment.

As I headed toward my mandatory retirement, I continued working a 100 percent schedule—maybe to squeeze every last moment out of a career I loved. My last major event was at the Players Championship in Florida, where PwC was a proud sponsor. One evening during the event, our CEO, together with the partner who would be my successor at the Governance Insights Center, held a lovely small and intimate retirement party for me, with maybe twenty to thirty colleagues and clients attending. My successor remarked that rarely, if ever, had she seen a partner who kept working at the pace I did through their last days with the firm. Our CEO remarked that one of the things he admired about me was the passion I brought to our clients, the firm, to everything I did. I cannot imagine two better compliments. That was who I was. It is still who I am.

The night before my retirement party, Mr. X. and I hosted a small dinner in New York for my close friends. Lu had been receiving cancer treatment at City of Hope but was able to come with her husband. I sat her next to Mr. X. that night and again the next night at the retirement party—both because of the importance of who she was in my life and how much I trusted her judgment. She had never met Mr. X., and if after spending substantive in-person time she liked and trusted him, it would almost be a form of insurance. After EB, I needed reassurance that what I was feeling and experiencing with this man was real and true and that it was safe for me to move forward with him in my life. After those two evenings, Lu gave him and the relationship her seal of approval.

That night, after the dinner, Mr. X. and I had sex for the first time. I don't know, maybe it was the alcohol, but it was good sex. Better than with my Cary Grant–handsome ex-husband. And then it got better and better. He may not have looked like a movie star, but Mr. X. was an incredibly attentive lover. Unlike with Evil Bastard, it was all about me.

***

The next night was my elegant, black-tie retirement party in a private room at Del Posto. It started with cocktails and passed hors d'oeuvres, followed by a four-course seated dinner. There were beautiful flower arrangements on each table and a classical guitarist. The entire evening was captured by a professional photographer. There were approximately seventy-five to eighty friends, colleagues, clients, and others in my business world, including Mr. G., who had once asked me about

Mr. X.'s "estranged wife." That night, Mr. X. and I told him we were engaged, and he was nothing but excited for us. Neither of us had told him we were dating. "Are you kidding?" he said. "That's wonderful!" The photographer captured that moment.

I spent the night surrounded by friends and colleagues who had been there for me, who had supported me and worked with me, who had helped me reach this place and achieve a type of success I'd never imagined or dreamed about. I felt overwhelmed with gratitude and so loved, encircled by the brilliant, talented, amazing, and kind people who were my friends.

And then, just like that, I was a retired partner. But not completely. I didn't consider myself "done" professionally. I was ready to begin my next chapter, hoping to find a position on corporate boards and continue on the boards of charitable organizations that were doing work I believed in.

Mr. X. and I had mutually agreed that 2015 was not the year to get married. I discussed this with Lu and Kellee, and both encouraged and advised us to wait until 2016 for a number of reasons. Finally, in February of 2016, with some help from Kellee, we picked a wedding date—August 13, 2016. It was a Saturday, but there was some discussion of the fact that our anniversary would occasionally fall on Friday the thirteenth. The weekend we decided, Mr. X. was in LA, his first time visiting me there. We hosted a dinner party at my apartment for two FOMAC couples. I remember a wonderful afternoon cooking together, talking about our future and how we would "keep it fresh," and choosing the day. We told my friends the plan and asked, "Does it bother any of you that some years our anniversary would be on Friday the thirteenth?" They all said, "We think it's great."

One couple were friends from Caltech I had known since my time with EB. The second couple, who I met on the East Coast in my last position with PwC, were both retired career military. Sometime after this, Couple Number Two were in New York City, and we went to the Met to see a special exhibit in the Egyptian wing. We were having lunch at the Met Dining Room when they said, "So tell us more about Mr. X." I don't recall what I said, but they looked at me and said, "Tell us about his wife."

I said, "Mr. X. has never been married."

They said, "Oh, okay" and dropped it, but the comment bothered me. This wasn't the first time I had heard something about Mr. X. having a wife. When I got back to my apartment, I googled Mr. X., and all that came up through several pages were the normal articles you would find about any successful business leader. There was nothing that mentioned a wife. So I typed in "Mr. X. (full name)" and "wife." With that I found a single article from many years prior about a gift to a charitable organization. The article talked about "Mr. X. and his wife Mrs. X."

I called him.

I told him what I had read. "Mr. X., what about this article? Who is Mrs. X?"

He told me she was his cousin.

That did not make sense to me. Why would the article refer to the woman as his wife? I pressed him to explain. He said it was just a silly mistake that he'd never bothered to correct. I somehow rationalized that the explanation made sense. I could find nothing else. There were no Google images of him with a Mrs. X.

The idea of Mr. X. having a wife just did not make sense. He was a successful businessman. When Hillary Clinton was running for president, he told me she'd called him, and we created this whole fantasy thinking that she might offer him an important position. This was a man who was going places … and I was going to be his wife.

Sometime shortly after this, my friends W. and M. included Mr. X. and me in a small dinner party at their Fifth Avenue apartment overlooking Central Park. We were in the living room having cocktails, gazing out at Central Park, a perfect New York fall evening. And W. said, "There's an apartment for sale in this building."

Mr. X. was immediately interested. W. mentioned that he was the president of the building's co-op and introduced us to Ms. R., one of the other guests at the dinner, who was a successful Realtor. The next thing I knew, we were apartment hunting in New York City, looking for the place we would call home. It was a phenomenal experience, like something out of a movie. Every apartment we looked at was either on Fifth Avenue or Central Park West, because we had very specific criteria, including that the apartment had to have a spectacular view, ideally of Central Park, but any fabulous city view would do. What mattered most to me was the floor plan, the bones of the place, and the building. I could figure out what could be done (or, more accurately, what Hugo and I could do) to make an apartment ours.

Eventually, we narrowed it down to four or five places, including the apartment that was in W.'s building. That unit was on the top floor, and while it had only a side view of Central Park from the dining room windows, it had beautiful city views and light. It also had a private staircase up to the roof deck that looked out to one of the reservoirs in Central Park. It was, essentially, a pinch-me-level Manhattan dream home.

Mr. X. made an offer that was accepted. We were introduced to a real estate attorney, and it appeared we were going full speed ahead to buy a Manhattan co-op. That meant we were embarking on an invasive and time-consuming process that involved full financial disclosure and references, all of which would go to the co-op board, which also interviewed the potential buyers. If a co-op board chose not to approve a potential buyer, they did not even have to tell you why. During a conversation, Mr. X. asked W., "Is it going to be a problem?"

"Is what going to be a problem?" asked W.

"Us," Mr. X. said, meaning him and me. He was worried that a mixed-race couple might be an issue for the board. W. assured him that it was not. Of course it was not. We were all over New York. Mr. X. once invited me to meet him in DC when he was attending a high-profile meeting. Riding Amtrak together from DC to New York City, we must have been a somewhat noticeable couple—a large Black man and a small white woman, both in their sixties, both of us recognizable in certain circles—we definitely were not something you see every day. On that train we sat in the first-class car holding hands. Anyone and everyone could have seen us. You never know who you're going to see on an Amtrak train between New York and DC. Even Joe Biden took Amtrak!

On this particular train ride, Mr. X. did not travel all the way to New York City with me. When we reached his stop, he got off, and I continued on.

I had never gone to Mr. X.'s home city or seen his house. But there was never any need for me to go there, was there? We were engaged. New York was, after all, New York, and him coming to me was the chivalrous thing to do. Sometimes we would stay at my studio apartment, and sometimes we would get a suite at one of New York City's most luxurious hotels. It was all very romantic. I felt very taken care of.

***

Some months before our wedding, things at one of Mr. X.'s boards started to blow up. One of his fellow board members accused him of insider trading, which forced the company to start an investigation. He had to get his own counsel and was represented by two partners at Ms. L.'s white-shoe law firm. I didn't say anything to Ms. L., but the next time she came to visit, Mr. X. was there, and he told her about the investigation. Ms. L. said, "If there's ever anything I can do to help, just let me know." Mr. X. did not tell her that two of her partners were representing him, so neither did I.

The case quickly got nasty, and it was exhausting for Mr. X. Despite the strain, we still went out whenever he could make it to New York, and we still enjoyed ourselves thoroughly. We had phenomenal meals in the city—and he continued to spend like money was no object. At one of our favorite places, the hostess said, "You are here all the time. You don't have to make a reservation. Just call me anytime, and I'll get you in." We knew the waiters, and they knew us. It was so much fun.

At some point, we learned from W. that one of our soon-to-be neighbors in our new apartment building was a billionaire, Mr. B., whom Mr. X. knew. "Mr. B. made me my first million dollars," he told me. He also said he was going to give Mr. B. a call.

Still, Mr. X. seemed to be dragging his feet as far as getting into our new home. I knew from Ms. R. that she had been pressuring Mr. X. to get some information to our real estate attorney, and she asked me for help. I explained that his business demands were extraordinary and that I would discuss it with him, and he responded, in writing, that he was working as hard as he could to "keep it moving apace." We had agreed to have Hugo come spend some time at the apartment so he could start the design process and be ready to go as soon as we closed. But when Hugo arrived, Mr. X. told me he would not be able to make it to the city as planned. Not only that—he had forgotten to check with Ms. R. and arrange for Hugo and me to visit the apartment. He apologized and said he would call and see if Ms. R. could meet us on short notice, but then he told me he'd had no luck setting it up. He told me he was going back and forth with the attorney to address various issues—he blamed the sellers, an estate with multiple parties involved. Ms. R. had told us there were issues with a potential buyer before us, so this was quite plausible. But our wedding day was coming up, and I was anxious for things to start falling into place.

Then one night in May, about three months before our August 13 wedding date, Mr. X. came to New York City, took me to dinner at the same neighborhood restaurant where he first told me he was courting me, and said he had something important to tell me.

"I have bladder cancer," he said, "and they think I may have prostate cancer too."

Mr. X. had been through bladder cancer before. Once a year, in the fall, he would go to Memorial Sloan Kettering for a screening. His last test a few months before had been negative, but apparently something had changed. And that seemed to be enough for Mr. X. He told me, "I'm not going to put you through this."

I thought he was telling me we could call it quits, that he would not marry me because his cancer was back.

I looked at him and said, "Mr. X., that is not me. We will get through this together." Then I said, "Let's get a second opinion. Let me call my internist friend at UCLA." He agreed and said he thought that was a good idea. Then he needed to go home. He was in the final throes of the insider trading investigation, and there was so much more he needed to do. He had a meeting scheduled with his attorneys the next morning. But I didn't want him to go. After what he had told me, I could not stand to see him leave. "Please don't go," I said. "Please stay."

That night may have been the best sex I've ever had in my life. Or that morning—I don't remember. Bladder cancer and all.

The next day, I sent a note to the internist who was a member of FOMAC. I explained that it had been only a few months since Mr. X.'s yearly screening, when everything had been fine. She wrote back that this was not uncommon. "Bladder cancer is one of those very insidious cancers," she explained, "and it can come back at any time." She asked for copies of his results and promised to check with someone at UCLA.

We had decided on a venue for our Los Angeles wedding, and before he left that morning, he gave me a copy of his credit card and signed the contract. We had planned a small but star-studded event. One night, I was having drinks with friends in the lobby of the midtown Manhattan Waldorf Astoria when Mr. X. came up behind me and said to me and my friends, "Guess what I found out today? I heard from George Benson (the famous jazz guitarist), and he's agreed to play at our wedding." He also said that Jimmy Carter, whom he told me he had a friendship with as much as one does with former presidents, was going to officiate. I could not believe it. The former president was going to marry us.

As the big day drew closer, I started to feel overwhelmed. There was so much to do. I sent Ms. L., the UCLA internist, and another friend an email saying, "You know how hard it is for me to ask anybody for anything. But I want to do something the night before the wedding for people coming in from out of town. Would you work together to host a small dinner party the night before the wedding? Because I don't think I can do it all."

Immediately, Ms. L. wrote back, "Hell yes!" The other friends did the same. They said they would have it catered at one of their homes.

Everything was coming together.

***

On a Friday afternoon, Ms. L. sent me a screenshot of a note that went out at her firm. The note was to let the firm's partners know that there was an article in a major newspaper about the investigation involving Mr. X. There were no names in the article. The note went on to advise that the firm represented a party in the matter and that any inquiries should be referred to the two partners handling it.

I wrote back, "Thanks for letting me know." I did not let on that I had known about it for months or that it was Mr. X. her partners were representing.

The following Monday afternoon, I got a text from Ms. L:

"Lu, Kellee, and I need to talk with you right away."

My immediate thought was that it was bad news about Lu. She was still seeing patients even as she continued treatment for the cancer, but … it would make sense that they would all want to tell me together.

Ms. L. set up a dial-in conference call, and I called the number. Everyone said hello, and I asked what was going on.

"Mary Ann," Ms. L. said, "there's no easy way to say this. Mr. X. is married."

CHAPTER 8

BETRAYAL

It had started unfolding with the Friday firm-wide note to partners at Ms. L.'s law firm. Once she learned her firm was representing someone in the company investigation Mr. X. had discussed with her a few months before, she emailed the partners in the firm communication to set up a call. I knew both her partners going back to my days with my former firm. When she talked with one of them Monday morning, she confirmed he knew me, and she told him she and I were good friends and that I was marrying a board member at the company that was the subject of the newspaper article. She wanted to know if a real or perceived conflict of interest could exist and asked if there was an issue with her hosting a party for us.

He responded, "Ms. L., how can Mr. X. be marrying Mary Ann when he's married to someone else?"

Ms. L. said, "What?"

"I've been in their home," her partner told her. "I've had drinks with Mr. X. and his wife in their home."

That was when she called Lu and Kellee, and they decided to set up the conference call to break the news.

Maybe this was why he never got around to buying me a ring.

***

Lu, Kellee, Ms. L., and I agreed that I needed to confront Mr. X., and we discussed what form that should take. Either Lu or Kellee suggested I call his wife. Kellee said she could get me her phone number that afternoon. I immediately said, "No, I won't do that." I have never, ever regretted that decision. I thought, *For what purpose?* I had no desire to hurt her. Had I known she existed, I never would have had a relationship with Mr. X.

I do not cry easily and did not that afternoon. I once again immediately went into business-transaction mode. Kellee has since come to describe me as "living with no exhaust." I went from planning a wedding to figuring out how to extricate myself from my situation. Our conversation moved to planning my "confrontation call" with Mr. X. What was I going to say? Of course, I was going to tell him I knew he had a wife. But after that, what did I want or need?

Mr. X. was different than EB, who mooched off me pretty much forever. Mr. X. had courted me. When we went out to dinner in New York, when we got a suite at a hotel instead of staying at my studio apartment, he always paid. He was a man in that respect.

But he didn't pay for *everything.* The businesswoman in me zeroed in on the fact that I had spent money based on promises that either had not been or could not be kept. For example, when I could not decide between two wedding dresses, Mr. X. told me to buy both and that he would pay for them. I never asked for reimbursement. It was the same with all the costs I had incurred for wedding preparations and in anticipation of moving into our Fifth Avenue apartment. I thought, *We're going to be married. It's all going to come out in the wash.* But this was no longer the case. So I decided that what I wanted was for Mr. X. to reimburse me for those costs.

***

Mr. X. could be hard to get hold of (a fact that suddenly made a lot more sense to me), so I texted him the following:

"Mr. X., something's come up. You and I need to talk this afternoon. It's critical. And if you can't talk, I'll arrange to be in your office later today."

He immediately texted me back, or he called me. I forget how we started, as well as everything else about the beginning of the conversation, up until the point I said, "Mr. X., I just found out you're married."

"Mary Ann," he said, "where is this coming from?"

"Ms. L."

"You and I have been through all that before," he said. "I told you she is my cousin."

I repeated, "Mr. X., I know you're married."

He was insistent. How could I believe that?

I told him about Ms. L. and her call with her partner, who was also Mr. X.'s counsel. I told him Ms. L.'s partner told her that Mr. X. was married.

Mr. X. asked how Ms. L.'s partner could possibly know or say that.

I told Mr. X. that Ms. L.'s partner knew that because he had been in Mr. X.'s house and met Mr. X.'s wife. And that he told all this to Ms. L., and Ms. L. told me.

Mr. X. continued to deny it.

I kept going over the facts, explaining that I knew Ms. L.'s partner had been to his house, that he had met his wife, that he'd told Ms. L. everything, that Ms. L. had told me. Not once, not twice, not three times. Over and over. He denied it all, every time. We went back and forth and back and forth. And then he finally said, "Oh, all right. So I'm married."

As if it was some sort of victory for me.

There was dead silence for a while. Then he asked me a question. At one point during the allegations against him and the resulting investigation, we had nicknamed one of his colleagues Evil Bastard 2, after my ex-husband. He asked me, "Does this mean I'm Evil Bastard 3?"

I wanted to say, "No, you're in a league all your own." But I said nothing.

I said nothing about a lot of things. I did not ask him what he expected would happen on August 13, if he intended to leave me standing at the altar, or go through with the wedding and commit bigamy, or fake his death. I certainly did not ask him why.

Instead, I said, "Mr. X., there were a number of costs that I incurred with your agreement, with your blessing, in anticipation of this wedding."

He indicated that he understood.

"I would like for you to reimburse me for those," I said.

"Okay."

I told him I would send him an email with an itemized list. Then we ended the call. In total, we were on the phone for about a half hour. But that is all I remember in terms of content. I suppose most of that time was spent going around in circles, just trying to get him to admit to the truth.

Later that day I made a list of the costs I felt he should reimburse. The total was over $13,000. I sent him an email that read something like "Dear Mr. X.: In anticipation of our August 13, 2016, wedding and life together, I incurred the following costs. Pursuant to our conversation, you have agreed to reimburse me for these costs." I used language that put on the record

a. that we had been engaged,

b. that we had a set wedding date,

c. that there were people who knew about it, and

d. that these were the expenses.

I did not attach receipts but offered to send them if he wanted. I closed with "I look forward to your prompt payment. Please let me know if you have questions. Mary Ann."

I do not remember if I copied his assistant. There were times during our relationship when I would copy her on things, just like I copied my assistant. It made coordinating our schedules easier, since we were both always traveling and busy. But at one point Mr. X. told me I didn't need to copy his assistant on everything. I get it now.

Still, she had to know there was something going on.

I waited a couple of weeks. I had not received a check, so I sent a follow-up message, reminding Mr. X. what he owed me, that he had agreed to pay it, and that the money had still not been received. I got a message back very, very promptly, with apologies, essentially saying the check was in the mail. And within days, it arrived. I think it came from his personal account, payable to me. He left the subject line blank, but he signed it.

I deposited the check. And I never saw or heard from him again.

***

I do not know why I was able to put Mr. X. behind me so easily, but I was. I was done. I guess I will give you my all, but once you have shown me who you are, that is it. The only thing left was for me to let my circle of wonderful friends know that there would be no August wedding. I sent emails that basically said some version of "There is no easy way to say this, but I found out Mr. X. is married. I immediately ended it. I am fine, and I will reach out to you if I need anything."

We were all in shock. And everyone kept asking those same questions: "What was he actually going to do? Had he planned to leave me standing at the altar, commit bigamy, or maybe fake his own funeral?" Who knows? Did he even know?

My friends almost seemed more upset than I was. For me, it was like a switch had turned off. Of course it hurt, but what really hurt was that I'd believed him. That as hard as I worked to guard my heart, it had happened to me again. But once I knew who Mr. X. was, I was done. There was no point in continuing. I was not losing anything, because I never really had anything. It was all a sham.

I did have some curiosity about Mr. X.'s wife and how he was able to keep her a secret. I asked an author friend, a much better researcher than I, to see what she could find out about Mrs. X. She got back to me and said, "I am the world's best Google researcher, and I am not convinced this woman exists. I cannot find out any more than you did. I cannot find a picture."

I knew Lu was concerned about me, and we set up a time to talk a few days after that Monday afternoon call. And I told her, "I am fine. You know I will reach out to you if I'm not." But I also said, "I was snookered again, Lu." Lu said, "Mary Ann, I was snookered too, and I'm a professional."

One set of friends, Mrs. and Mr. C. who lived in New Jersey, came into the city to see me. Mrs. C. and I took a walk in Central Park and later met Mr. C. for dinner. The moment I saw Mrs. C., I fell into her arms and burst into tears. "I feel so stupid," I said, hugging her. She just said, "Mary Ann, don't. Don't." I now realize that what really upset me and made me angry was not that Mr. X. had snookered me but rather how dare he bring my friends into it? I remember at my retirement party feeling this incredible protective sense of all these people around me, encircling me like a fortress. Maybe that is where I got the strength to pivot and move on. I had all that love with me, surrounding me. Compared to what I had in my life, Mr. X.'s fake love meant nothing. Plus, karma would get him. It always does. At least, I believe it does.

And I believe it has and will continue for Mr. X. Long after all this happened, one of those friends from my retirement party and I saw an announcement that he had landed a spot on a corporate board alongside a friend of hers. She had been particularly disgusted with Mr. X.'s behavior and called this friend and told him all about Mr. X. and me and his secret wife. Everyone operates under a different set of morals, but she, her friend, and I all share the view that you are who you are and that if you lack morals and a conscience, that is likely not isolated to your personal life. What Mr. X. had done showed who he was.

I know that this friend of my friend asked her for specifics, and she asked me, and I provided them, including copies of emails and the note he had given me when he proposed.

I know only a small part of what happened next, and even this I heard only thirdhand, but it sounded to me like Mr. X., when confronted, had a similar response to the one he'd had with me. There was nothing to it. It was not true. It was deny, deny, deny, deny, deny … until he could not deny it anymore, thanks to the evidence in front of him. At which point he finally gave up and said, "Oh, well—all right, I did it."

Which were almost the exact same words he'd used with me.

Lu always told me that the one thing people without a conscience fear most is being unmasked, people finding out who they really are. Maybe that is why Mr. X. fought so hard to keep up the facade.

Sometime after the split with Mr. X., I had an incredibly vivid dream. It was so intense it felt like more than a dream. In it, I was at an event, watching someone on stage. I was sitting in the front row, and Donald Trump, who was a presidential candidate at the time, was sitting next to me, on my right.

Trump looked at me and said, "I'm not hard for you to understand, Mary Ann. You know who I am. You've seen it from the beginning, because you have been with men like me." When I woke up, I realized he'd essentially told me I had seen how people without a conscience operate—what they can do and how they do it. "You know who I am. Why would you be surprised about anything that I say or do?" I'll never forget it. It was so vivid and so clear. I also remembered something Lu told me more than once: "They lie even when they don't have to."

***

I told W. and M. in person. I asked them to join me for dinner and started the conversation the same way Ms. L. had started the conversation with me and the way I was starting all these conversations. "There's no easy way to say this …" I told them everything, that Mr. X. was married, that we were done, and that I had been duped yet again. W. looked at me and told me he wasn't surprised. After Mr. X. told W. that he knew the billionaire Mr. B., W. called Mr. B. and told him that Mr. X. and I would soon be his neighbors. Mr. B.'s response was "Gee, W., I'm surprised Mr. X. can afford an apartment in our building."

I do not know whether or not he knew Mr. X. was married. But clearly it was all a con. The dinners, the people we met together, our friends, the engagement, the apartment, the wedding plans. All of it.

***

If there was one thing I was sure about, it was that I wanted to stay in Manhattan.

I sent Ms. R., Mr. X.'s and my Realtor, an email that said what was by then my standard "I found out Mr. X. is married, and we're done" message. I was embarrassed beyond words. Mr. X. had led her on as much as he'd led everyone else on, but in her case, it was also her occupation. He'd tied up the apartment for so long, playing whatever game he was playing with me, Ms. R., the real estate attorney, and with my friends. But Ms. R. was friends with W. and M., and the reality was that I needed a place to live. I told her I wanted to buy an apartment in New York, and while I did not expect her to work with someone with my (considerably smaller) budget, I asked if there might be someone she could refer me to who could help.

She graciously offered to be my Realtor again.

This time, instead of looking at classic sixes on Central Park West and Fifth Avenue, we were looking for a one-bedroom uptown or midtown in east or west Manhattan. I wanted to be in a full-service prewar building, which if you do not know New York means a building built before World War II—the classic buildings you often see in movies about New York. I did not care if the apartment was ugly or outdated, but again I cared about the floor plan and character of the place and what I could do with it. Or what Hugo could do with it. Ms. R. understood this. I understood that even though there were not a lot of must-haves on my list, I still might not get them all. We looked at a few places, and at first, even with my abbreviated wish list, it was discouraging. But then Ms. R. called me and said there was a unit available in Beekman Place and that once I saw it, I would have to make a decision that day or the day after.

I did not even know where Beekman Place was.

It turned out Beekman Place is, in fact, one of those classic New York neighborhoods near the UN in Midtown East. For movie lovers, Auntie Mame lived at 3 Beekman Place, and in *The Way We Were*, Barbra Streisand tells Robert Redford, "I don't fit in on Beekman Place. That's what's really wrong." It was a prewar full-service building, designed by an architect from that time period important enough that his name is noted in the listing. The building itself was lovely, and it had a splendid roof deck. The apartment itself was anything but lovely or splendid. Most people would walk in and think, *This is a disaster and I cannot imagine living here—let's move on to the next place.* Luckily, Ms. R. knew I did not need the place to be pretty to see what I could do with it. I fell in love with the building. I fell in love with the floor plan of the apartment. I texted Hugo, he gave his approval, and I made an offer that day.

So, I quickly closed, moved in, and lived happily ever after in my Manhattan dream home, right? Not exactly. Nothing in New York real estate is ever that easy. I knew that going in. The lease on the Upper West Side studio ran through the following June. I remember thinking, *What's the worst thing that could happen? I own it for a year and don't live in it.* It turns out that's exactly what happened. I made the offer in August. I had my board interview in November. I closed in December. That meant I was ready to start the renovations—except in New York you have to get everything approved by multiple parties. Plus, renovations had to be scheduled, because only a limited number of construction projects are allowed in an apartment building at one time. As a result, it was July of 2017—almost a year after my offer was accepted—before renovations started. The plan to have Hugo stay in the studio when he needed to be in New York City to manage the project fell apart. I was able to stay in LA much of the time, and I had several trips, but I also spent several weeks staying in New York City hotels as I waited for my new home to be ready—because I had a life in Manhattan and needed and wanted to be here. My first night in the apartment was in December 2017. And it was a few months after that before I could call it done.

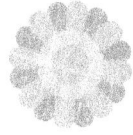

CHAPTER 9

HOME

While my life in New York was taking off, my dear friend Lu's life in Los Angeles was, sadly, coming to an end. The last time I saw her in person was at a Fourth of July party in LA in 2017. She was still working, still living her life. But she looked so frail. I do not know how or why, but I knew in my heart that it was the last time I would ever see her.

A few months later, I had the privilege of a backstage post-performance visit with a tremendous actress who was very, very close to Lu. I asked when she had last talked with Lu and in some way communicated that I was concerned that Lu would not be with us much longer. She seemed genuinely baffled by my comment. In her mind, Lu was fine. I believe that was the image Lu projected to virtually everyone, maybe even to herself. She was a strong woman, and she was determined to enjoy what life she had to the fullest.

Kellee and I were in close contact. I knew Lu was steadily declining and surrounded by her family and receiving the best care possible, and there was nothing I could do to make it better. I trusted that Kellee would tell me if I could have done anything for Lu or her, and I would have been on the next plane to Los Angeles. But apart from that, I did not want to interrupt the process or disrupt any of her time with her family. She had already given me so much. And we had a connection that did not require being in the same physical space.

Lu died in April 2018, surrounded by her family, the way she wanted. I will forever be grateful for her friendship.

***

PwC has a top-quality transition program for partners approaching retirement. The program is designed to help partners and their spouses or significant others be better prepared to move from the life of a busy, sought-after corporate executive with an all-consuming job into whatever comes next. A big part of the process is helping identify what comes next. The program involves reflection and sharing with the group. When it was my turn to fess up and tell everybody what I wanted to do with my post-partnership life, I admitted something that was hard to say out loud, even to myself. I wanted to write a book. I also wanted it to be good. I am here writing this now in an attempt to make as good on that promise as I can.

Still, my postretirement plan was not simply to hole up in my (admittedly fabulous!) apartment and write. I also wanted to remain engaged and relevant. So, I chose to continue to maintain a presence in the business world. I was asked and agreed to join several corporate boards, all a little bit different, all of which require different amounts of time on any given day, depending on what is going on. Sometimes they require more energy than at other times or than I wish they did, and sometimes I lose sleep because I am still dealing with the pressures of professional life. But that is a choice. I also serve on a few charitable boards, all in Los Angeles, including the Geffen Playhouse. So, in addition to New York, I still very much have a life and close friends on the West Coast.

I never feared retirement. I do not know what I would have done or how long I would have stayed if there had not been mandatory retirement at age sixty. But I always knew that I was not going to be bored. I do not know that I have ever been bored in my life, never thought, *What am I going to do with my time?* To me, it's more like *There's so much I want to do, and there is never enough time to do it.*

I remember being at an event once, playing one of those get-to-know-you games around the table, and somebody asked the question, "If you could do anything you wanted, what would it be?" My answer was "Continuous learning." To me, living a good life means always being in the process of learning something new. I wish I had come up with the idea myself, but it came from someone I met at W. and M.'s one night at dinner. He said, "My goal is that if I die in the afternoon, I hope I learned something new that morning." That resonated with me. Especially since I am lucky enough to live in this magical city full of endless opportunities to learn and do. So I keep learning and doing. I decided I wanted to learn French, so once a week, I take French lessons. I will never be good at it, but that doesn't stop me from working on it.

I've always liked art, and working with Hugo unleashed a passion for it. New York City offers countless opportunities for continuous learning on that front. I can easily visit the Metropolitan Museum of Art, the Museum of Modern Art (MoMA), the Frick, the Guggenheim, or the American Museum of Natural History, just to name a few, to see special exhibits or the permanent collections. Programs are regularly offered where I can join a small group for a lecture presented by a curator. That's part of what makes New York so amazing. Anything you might be interested in, the opportunities for learning are endless.

I have had some incredible experiences through my memberships at these museums, like private previews and tours and parties, and have also been privileged to meet and spend time with many people in the art world, some of whom have become good friends. Go figure.

Recently, a friend commented that the pandemic must have been a horrible experience for me. It's funny. Even though he is a good friend who has known me for a long time, he thinks, maybe because I am always doing something, that I am an extrovert. I am very much the opposite. I don't fault him for his assumption. A lot of people think that about me, because so much of my career has involved meeting and interacting with people. So yes, I am perfectly comfortable getting up and speaking to a room of five hundred people, holding my own in a contentious meeting full of important executives, or hosting and/or attending events and parties. I do all that, and do it well. I much prefer small, intimate dinners or outings where I can really talk with people, have meaningful conversations, build real relationships—that is what has always mattered to me.

My professional and personal life has taken me on a journey where I have met and continue to meet wonderful people of all ages, forming relationships that, to paraphrase the opening lines of a poem by Brian A. Chalker, have come into my life for "a reason, a season, or a lifetime." I am blessed and grateful to be surrounded by friends who are the best of humanity and interesting, an eclectic group that includes businesspeople, scientists, medical professionals, people who have served in all branches of the military, artists, writers, thespians, singers, and songwriters. That is where my life has taken me.

So, when the pandemic hit, I did not feel cut off from the world. First, I was still working. The boards I served on were still meeting and still doing business, all while facing a whole new set of issues. I found it fascinating that, as a world, we turned on a dime and found new ways to get what needed to get done, done. Not that I considered Zoom a solution to every pandemic problem. When it came to Zoom cocktail hours, there were less than a handful for which I would ever log on. Zoom felt too much like work. Instead, I much preferred pouring a glass of wine or mixing a cocktail and heading down to the third floor of my building for a socially distanced cocktail hour with my dear friends and neighbors, Scott and Karen. They would sit in their doorway, and I would sit six feet away in the hall, and we would drink and chat. There was a fun, absurdist element to the whole thing. It seems silly now, given what we know about COVID-19, but at the time it made sense.

Honestly, spending the pandemic in New York City was almost— odd as it might sound—a magical experience. If you do not live here, you probably saw the news coverage of the way the entire city pulled together, cheering for our healthcare workers every night. I felt privileged to be able to share such a unique and powerful experience with my neighbors. I felt proud to be a New Yorker. Then, in late August or early September, the museums finally opened. It was incredible— there were no tourists in Manhattan, and they were limiting capacity because of social distancing. I put on my mask and walked up to the Met or the few blocks from my apartment to MoMA. At MoMA I rode the usually crowded escalators with nobody else in sight—just me, the security guard, and maybe one other person. I told myself, *Okay, this is not good, because the reason this is happening is because of this horrible disease that is killing people.* But another part of me was in heaven. *This is glorious, because I am in a museum and there are no other people around. It's magnificent.* The whole city was like that. You could walk up or down Fifth Avenue, which is normally tourist hell, and it was sparse, and you knew that everyone you saw lived there.

Like I said, even in a pandemic, it really was magical.

***

Since the pandemic ended, I've discovered a new passion—ballroom dancing. I was sharing a car with a fellow board member after a meeting, and he mentioned that his wife was really into ballroom dancing. He told me she took lessons and was an amateur competitor. I asked if he was her dance partner, and he said, "Oh, heavens no. She goes to the Fred Astaire studio on the Upper West Side. If you ever want an introduction, we know the owners ..."

It was as if a lightbulb went off for me. Until that moment, it had not occurred to me to pursue ballroom dancing as a single person. I wanted very much to try it myself. Still, I knew there was no way I was going to regularly go over to the Upper West Side. One day I went online and found a Fred Astaire studio a few blocks away from my apartment. I signed up for an introductory lesson, which was on September 24, 2022. Since then, the only weeks I have not taken one—and often several—lessons are when I am traveling.

I walk eleven blocks to the studio and enter a completely different world, one that is a community I am now part of. The studio is owned by former champion professional dance partners Tina and Plamen. All the instructors are former or current professional competitive dancers, which means they are also phenomenal athletes. My instructor, Robin, and his partner in dance and in life, Diana, who also teaches at the studio, are currently competing and winning, on their way up. They are a beautiful couple—inside and out—talented and exquisite dancers, a joy to watch. All have become an important part of my life. For an hour and a half, which is the length of my lesson, I tune out the world and focus on the beauty of dance. It is therapy in every way—for the mind, the body, and the soul.

I have no desire to compete, but the perfectionist in me wants to be good, to progress. I have performed with Robin several times in front of an audience, although I have yet to invite any of my friends to come and watch. But some people do, and that is when you can see some of the most beautiful moments of this community happen.

At one such event, an older, widowed gentleman danced with Tina. He and I are often at the studio at the same time for lessons. He comes in with his walker but puts it aside as Tina takes him to the dance floor. At this event, after they had danced several numbers and before he left, Tina stood arm in arm with him and addressed everyone. "I want to share something," she said. "I first met Ed and his wife over twenty years ago, soon after I came to this studio. After Ed lost his wife, he has continued to come and dance. He's ninety-eight years old." She was crying as she pointed out his son and grandson, who were sitting in the audience cheering him on. And Ed was fabulous. If that is not a testament to the magic of what dance can do, I don't know what is. It was a joy to be there that evening, to see him on the dance floor, to witness the connection and caring, and to be part of this community, filled with love, support, and the beauty of dance.

***

I often walk down the streets of New York and pinch myself that this is my life. How could this have possibly happened? How did a mother-less girl from a tiny town in the middle of nowhere wind up with this big, full, incredible life, with homes in LA and New York City, with a passport stamped with countries on every continent, with a career that still has me interacting with the most interesting people in science, medicine, business, theater, and museums? How could this be me?

I had a conversation with my brother that really struck me. He lost his wife to cancer in October 2022, and in December of that year, I was in Texas visiting with him and his two daughters. The older one was getting ready for her May 2023 wedding, and the younger one had a serious boyfriend. We were talking about family, and he mentioned that both his daughters' partners came from broken families. He commented that this was so different from him and his late wife, because they both came from "two-parent, *normal* homes."

I did not say anything. But what a statement about how different our family experiences were, despite our being brother and sister. Still, while he was the one raised with all the comforts of a "normal" family, I somehow was able to achieve everything I have achieved and do everything I have done without that foundation. My childhood did not break me.

Maybe it actually made me.

I cannot say for sure. I do not know what those early lessons taught me. Was it a combination of the values I learned from my father—those values of empathy, acceptance, and openness to learning that at the same time made me not fit in where I was? Was it some sort of strength of character I saw in my grandparents? I still have no idea.

If there is anything I can put my finger on, it is that I always wanted more than just survival. I knew that I wanted to *live*. I had no idea what living meant or what I was supposed to do to get there other than work hard and stay true to my values. But it also meant that whenever I saw a door open, I walked through it. There is a great line from *The Sound of Music,* when Maria has returned to the convent and the Mother Superior insists she go back to the von Trapp family. The Mother Superior tells her—and Maria repeats as she is leaving— "When the Lord closes a door, somewhere he opens a window." I think that is how I have lived my life. Throughout my life, opportunities have presented themselves. Doors and windows have opened for me. *Why should I go through it? I don't know. But there's a reason it showed up here, and I need to do this. I'll figure it out as I go.* So I did it, even if I was afraid. And after Evil Bastard, I was no longer afraid of anything.

Discussing a play that stirred up some racial controversy, a friend commented on a call, which included others, that it was hard to sit in the audience as a Black person and see white people cheering on certain elements of the play. I sent her an email that told her I appreciated her being so open and honest to share that, because it was not something I would have thought about. But I also told her that when I saw the play, even though I was one of those white people in the audience, I could relate to it in so many ways because I'd come from nothing and because I had close friends who had been victims of spousal abuse. I received a lovely message back, letting me know that she appreciated that I was able to share my perspective without challenging or judging her. She said, "I love that you'll always openly talk about things." That's a gift I've been given. I can only be here because of everything I've been through.

Maybe there was an upside to growing up with an absolute lack of privilege. Not just growing up without a lot of material comforts, but beyond that, growing up without that basic foundation a child gets from knowing they are loved and wanted by their parents. Maybe that is why I have always regarded every kindness, every beautiful moment, every good thing that happens to me, however small, as a gift. I grew up with absolutely no expectations. I expected nothing to be given to me, because nothing ever was.

Among my blessings are my nieces and nephews, most by choice. Some have babies and young children of their own, and I see the boundless joy they are experiencing with their families. How lucky I am that they share this with me. This includes Trudi, to whom this book is dedicated, and niece by choice Jen, who is also my personal trainer. One day as I was walking home after working out with Jen, I found myself wondering, *Did anyone ever get joy from me as a baby, a toddler, a young girl?* I am not sure they did.

I am addicted to awe. I first heard those words from a professor on a Caltech Associates trip to Italy. When I researched the expression, I found a 2017 article by Sam Woolfe titled "Addicted to Awe." He notes that in the novel *Contact*, Carl Sagan coined the phrase *wonder junkie*. These expressions beautifully capture how I feel, because I am a wonder junkie, addicted to awe.

So the world never loses its power to surprise me, maybe because I've never lost the audacity to wonder. And as long as I'm privileged to walk this beautiful planet full of wonderful people and experiences, I never will.

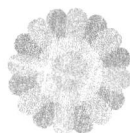

Mary Ann Cloyd is a seasoned and passionate business executive, currently serving as a director on several boards. As a PwC partner for twenty-five years, she held numerous leadership roles, including serving on both the Global and US Boards of Partners and Principals and as Leader of the Southern California, Phoenix, and Las Vegas tax practices. Her last position before retiring in 2015 was leading PwC's Governance Insights Center, championing the firm's external governance initiatives.

Mary Ann's warmth and dedication extend beyond her professional life. She is deeply involved in community organizations, currently serving as Vice Chair on the Board of Directors of the Geffen Playhouse, on the Caltech Associates Board, and on the UCLA Iris Cantor Women's Center Advisory Board. She has previously served on the Boards of the PwC Charitable Foundation, California Chamber of Commerce, American Red Cross Southern California, and Junior Achievement of Southern California. Mary Ann graduated Summa Cum Laude from Baylor University with a Bachelor of Business Administration. She currently resides in the vibrant city of New York, bringing her energy and commitment to everything she does.

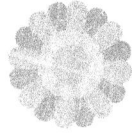

ACKNOWLEDGMENTS

With gratitude and love to:

Dr. Charlene Spoede Budd. For the inspiration you have been since I first took your class at Baylor, someone who has been through loss that no parent should ever have to experience and yet has gone on. And for being the first person, back in the late 1980s or early 1990s to recognize and tell me that I "had a book in me."

All of FOMAC (Friends of Mary Ann Cloyd) on both coasts, in between and across the Pond. I believe that people are in our lives for a reason, a season, or a lifetime, and there are members of FOMAC who were there even before I was MAC. For those with whom I have lost touch or with whom I have not had a chance to catch up in way too long, my gratitude is heartfelt—even if our time together was only for a reason or a season.

Lisa Canfield, with whom I worked closely to make this book a reality. It would not have happened without you.

Lu Katzman Staenberg, for your encouragement and insistence that I write this book, and for your love and friendship. I continue to feel it, even though you are no longer of this world.

Kellee White, you were there with your mom and me. I know as she keeps watch over both of us, it gives her joy to see that we look out for one another, and that you continued encouraging me to get this book done.

Trudi Cloyd, Donna, and Steve Chisolm. You were among the very few whose opinions I asked when I was in the go/no-go decision to move forward with the project. You did not hesitate for a moment in encouraging me to do so

My dear friend Carla Malden. You were the one whose opinion mattered most, the only one with whom I shared the outline, both because I respect your opinion as a talented author and because I knew you would be honest with me. And while it is your encouragement that was the final push, what matters most is your friendship, your understanding, and always being there for me ... know that I am always there for you.

.

www.ingramcontent.com/pod-product-compliance
Lightning Source LLC
Chambersburg PA
CBHW021235090426
42740CB00006B/538